The Diabetic Air Fryer Cookbook 2024

The Complete Guide To Managing Type 1 & 2 Diabetes Using Super Easy & Healthy Air-Frying Recipes | No-stress 30-Day Meal Plan

Letty L. Sears

Copyright© 2024 By Letty L. Sears
All Rights Reserved

This book is copyright protected. It is only for personal use.
You cannot amend, distribute, sell, use,
quote or paraphrase any part of the content within this book,
without the consent of the author or publisher.
Under no circumstances will any blame or
legal responsibility be held against the publisher,
or author, for any damages, reparation,
or monetary loss due to the information contained within this book,
either directly or indirectly.

Disclaimer Notice:
Please note the information contained within this
document is for educational and entertainment purposes only.
All effort has been executed to present accurate,
up to date, reliable, complete information.
No warranties of any kind are declared or implied.
Readers acknowledge that the author is not engaged
in the rendering of legal,
financial, medical or professional advice.
The content within this book has been derived from various sources.
Please consult a licensed professional before attempting any
techniques outlined in this book.
By reading this document,
the reader agrees that under no circumstances is the
author responsible for any losses,
direct or indirect,
that are incurred as a result of the use of the
information contained within this document, including,
but not limited to, errors, omissions, or inaccuracies.

Contents

Introduction	1
Chapter 1: Managing Diabetes	2
Chapter 2: Why Choose Air Fryers?	5
Chapter 3: Breakfast Recipes	9
Air Fryer Veggie Omelette	9
Crispy Turkey Bacon	9
Low-Carb Breakfast Burritos	9
Air-Fried Avocado and Egg	10
Cinnamon Apple Chips	10
Sweet Potato Hash Browns	10
Low-Carb French Toast Sticks	10
Zucchini Fritters	11
Air Fryer Breakfast Sausages	11
Spinach and Feta Egg Muffins	11
Cauliflower Hash Browns	12
Crispy Tofu Scramble	12
Almond Flour Pancakes	12
Low-Carb Sausage Balls	13
Egg and Veggie Breakfast Wraps	13
Air-Fried Breakfast Quinoa	13
Turkey and Egg Breakfast Cups	14
Low-Carb Cheese and Bacon Biscuits	14
Crispy Kale Chips	14
Breakfast Stuffed Peppers	15
Coconut Flour Waffles	15
Aubergine and Tomato Breakfast Stack	15
Cottage Cheese Pancakes	15
Air-Fried Breakfast Potatoes	16
Low-Carb Breakfast Pizza	16
Chapter 4: Main Recipes	17
Air-Fried Lemon Herb Chicken Breasts	17
Turkey Meatballs with Marinara Sauce	17
Cajun Seasoned Air-Fried Shrimp	17
Garlic Parmesan Air-Fried Chicken Wings	18

Herbed Pork Tenderloin Medallions	18
Teriyaki Glazed Salmon Fillets	18
Air-Fried Italian Sausage with Peppers and Onions	18
Paprika and Cumin Spiced Air-Fried Lamb Chops	19
Chili-Lime Air-Fried Chicken Thighs	19
Rosemary and Garlic Air-Fried Steak	19
Honey Mustard Glazed Air-Fried Pork Chops	20
Mediterranean Style Air-Fried Lamb Kebabs	20
Asian-Style Sesame Ginger Air-Fried Beef Stir-Fry	20
BBQ Pulled Chicken Sliders	21
Spicy Air-Fried Turkey Breast	21
Lemon Pepper Air-Fried Cod Fillets	21
Buffalo-Style Air-Fried Turkey Wings	21
Tandoori Chicken Skewers	22
Garlic and Herb Marinated Air-Fried Pork Tenderloin	22
Italian Seasoned Air-Fried Meatballs	22
Crispy Air-Fried Coconut Shrimp	23
Moroccan Spiced Air-Fried Chicken Drumsticks	23
Honey Sriracha Glazed Air-Fried Turkey Meatloaf	23
Jamaican Jerk Air-Fried Chicken Thighs	24
Paprika-Rubbed Air-Fried Beef Sirloin Tips	24
Air-Fried Stuffed Peppers with Quinoa and Black Beans	24
Crispy Tofu and Vegetable Stir-Fry in Air Fryer	25
Courgette Parmesan in the Air Fryer	25
Spinach and Mushroom Stuffed Portobello Mushrooms	25
Air-Fried Falafel with Tahini Sauce	26
Butternut Squash and Chickpea Curry in the Air Fryer	26
Caprese-Stuffed Air-Fried Courgette Boats	26
Air-Fried Veggie Burger Patties with Sweet Potato Fries	27
Mexican-Style Air-Fried Stuffed Poblano Peppers	27
Air-Fried Cauliflower Steaks with Herbed Quinoa Pilaf	27

Chapter 5: Fish and Seafood 28

Lemon Herb Air-Fried Tilapia Fillets	28
Cajun Spiced Air-Fried Shrimp Skewers	28
Garlic Butter Air-Fried Scallops	28
Teriyaki Glazed Air-Fried Salmon Steaks	28
Crispy Coconut-Crusted Air-Fried Cod Fillets	29
Herbed Lemon Air-Fried Swordfish Steaks	29
Panko-Crusted Air-Fried Haddock Fillets	29

Mediterranean Style Air-Fried Sea Bass 29
Lemon Pepper Air-Fried Catfish Nuggets 30
Blackened Air-Fried Red Snapper 30
Chili-Lime Air-Fried Shrimp Tacos 30
Honey Mustard Glazed Air-Fried Trout Fillets 31
Cajun Seasoned Air-Fried Crawfish 31
Parmesan Crusted Air-Fried Oysters 31
Sriracha-Glazed Air-Fried Mahi-Mahi 31
Herb-Marinated Air-Fried Scampi 32
Crispy Sesame Ginger Air-Fried Tuna Steaks 32
Coconut Lime Air-Fried Shrimp and Pineapple Skewers 32
Garlic Parmesan Air-Fried Crab Cakes 33
Spicy Chipotle Air-Fried Lobster Tails 33
Lemon-Herb Air-Fried Mussels 33
Dill and Garlic Air-Fried Squid Rings 33

Chapter 6: Poultry & Meat Recipes 34

Honey Garlic Air-Fried Chicken Thighs 34
Lemon Herb Air-Fried Turkey Breast 34
Teriyaki Glazed Air-Fried Duck Breast 34
BBQ Rubbed Air-Fried Pork Ribs 34
Cajun Spiced Air-Fried Quail 35
Paprika and Rosemary Air-Fried Lamb Chops 35
Buffalo-Style Air-Fried Chicken Tenders 35
Garlic Parmesan Air-Fried Turkey Meatballs 35
Moroccan Spiced Air-Fried Lamb Kebabs 35
Jamaican Jerk Air-Fried Pork Tenderloin 36
Herbed Air-Fried Cornish Hens 36
Chili-Lime Air-Fried Beef Skewers 36
Maple Mustard Glazed Air-Fried Ham Steaks 36
Crispy Orange-Glazed Air-Fried Duck Legs 36
Mediterranean Style Air-Fried Lamb Burgers 37
Honey Sriracha Air-Fried Chicken Wings 37
Rosemary Balsamic Air-Fried Beef Roast 37
Italian Herb Air-Fried Veal Cutlets 37
Pesto Marinated Air-Fried Chicken Drumsticks 38
Sesame Ginger Air-Fried Turkey Burgers 38
Lemon Pepper Air-Fried Rabbit 38
Soy-Garlic Marinated Air-Fried Pork Belly Slices 38

Chapter 7: Beans & Legumes 39

Air-Fried Spiced Chickpea Stuffed Peppers 39
Air-Fried Black Bean and Quinoa Burgers 39
Mediterranean Style Air-Fried Lentil Patties 39
Air-Fried Adzuki Beans with Herbs and Garlic 39
Cajun Cornbread-Coated Air-Fried Black Eyed Peas 40
Smoky Paprika Air-Fried Kidney Beans 40
Turmeric and Cumin Spiced Air-Fried Falafel 40
Air-Fried Mung Bean Sprouts Salad 40
Crispy Garlic Parmesan Air-Fried White Beans 41
Harissa Roasted Air-Fried Lima Beans 41
Herbed Chickpea Fritters in the Air Fryer 41
Air-Fried Split Pea Falafel with Tahini Sauce 41
Sesame Soy Air-Fried Soybean Sprouts 42
Air-Fried Black Bean and Sweet Potato Tacos 42
Pesto Marinated Air-Fried Cannellini Beans 42
Air-Fried Refried Beans with Chipotle 42
Spicy Curry Air-Fried Adzuki Bean Snack 43
Rosemary and Lemon Air-Fried Chickpea Salad 43
Air-Fried Lentil and Spinach Stuffed Mushrooms 43
Crunchy BBQ Seasoned Air-Fried Navy Beans 43

Chapter 8: Healthy Vegetables and Sides 44

Crispy Air-Fried Brussels Sprouts with Balsamic Glaze 44
Garlic Parmesan Air-Fried Green Beans 44
Air-Fried Asparagus Wrapped in Prosciutto 44
Turmeric Spiced Air-Fried Cauliflower Steaks 44
Herbed Air-Fried Carrot Fries 44
Panko-Crusted Air-Fried Courgette Chips 45
Air-Fried Stuffed Mushrooms with Spinach and Feta 45
Chili-Lime Air-Fried Corn on the Cob 45
Paprika Roasted Air-Fried Broccoli Florets 45
Lemon Herb Air-Fried Artichoke Hearts 46
Balsamic Glazed Air-Fried Aubergine Slices 46
Parmesan Crusted Air-Fried Acorn Squash Rings 46
Herb-Marinated Air-Fried Tomato Slices 46
Crispy Garlic-Parmesan Air-Fried Okra 47
Turmeric and Cumin Roasted Air-Fried Radishes 47
Crispy Air-Fried Butternut Squash Cubes 47

Buffalo Cauliflower Bites in the Air Fryer 47
Rosemary Roasted Air-Fried Pepper Strips 47
Lemon-Pepper Air-Fried Sugar Snap Peas 48
Air-Fried Ratatouille Medley 48
Garlic-Herb Air-Fried Parsnip Fries 48
Sesame Ginger Air-Fried Bok Choy 48
Herb-Marinated Air-Fried Cabbage Wedges 49
Crispy Parmesan-Rosemary Air-Fried Potatoes 49
Mediterranean Style Air-Fried Green Bean Salad 49
Honey Sriracha Glazed Air-Fried Carrot Coins 49

Chapter 9: Fast and Easy Everyday Favourites 50

Air-Fried Lemon Pepper Chicken Thighs 50
Crispy Air-Fried Veggie Spring Rolls 50
BBQ Rubbed Air-Fried Pork Loin Slices 50
Air-Fried Honey Mustard Turkey Breast 50
Teriyaki Glazed Air-Fried Tofu Steaks 51
Herbed Air-Fried Chicken Drumettes 51
Air-Fried Beef and Pepper Skewers 51
Parmesan-Herb Air-Fried Tilapia Fillets 51
Buffalo Cauliflower Florets in the Air Fryer 52
Pesto Marinated Air-Fried Shrimp Scampi 52
Crispy Tofu Nuggets in the Air Fryer 52
Air-Fried Italian Sausage and Veggie Stir-Fry 52
Lemon Herb Air-Fried Salmon Steaks 52
Mediterranean Style Air-Fried Aubergine Slices 53
Air-Fried Turkey and Spinach Meatballs 53
Coconut-Crusted Air-Fried Shrimp Cakes 53
Garlic-Rosemary Air-Fried Potato Wedges 53
Air-Fried Falafel Patty Burgers 54
Spicy Soy-Glazed Air-Fried Tofu Cubes 54
Lemon Garlic Air-Fried Cod Fillets 54

Chapter 10: Appetisers 55

Crispy Air-Fried Courgette Fries with Yoghurt Dip 55
Air-Fried Stuffed Jalapeño Poppers with Cream Cheese 55
Parmesan-Crusted Air-Fried Cauliflower Bites 55
Garlic-Herb Air-Fried Mushrooms Stuffed with Spinach and Cheese 56
Air-Fried Buffalo Chicken Wings with Greek Yoghurt Ranch Dip 56
Crispy Coconut Shrimp with Mango Dipping Sauce 56

Lemon Pepper Air-Fried Artichoke Hearts 56
Spicy Sriracha Air-Fried Tofu Bites 57
Mediterranean Style Air-Fried Falafel with Tahini Sauce 57
Crispy Onion Rings in the Air Fryer with Spicy Aioli 57
Teriyaki Glazed Air-Fried Meatballs 58
Herbed Air-Fried Potato Skins with Turkey Bacon 58
Cajun Spiced Air-Fried Okra Fritters 58
Air-Fried Stuffed Cherry Tomatoes with Herbed Goat Cheese 59
Pesto Mozzarella-Stuffed Air-Fried Portobello Mushrooms 59
Garlic Parmesan Air-Fried Green Beans...59
Crispy Thai-Style Air-Fried Spring Rolls with Dipping Sauce 59
Air-Fried Greek Spanakopita Triangles 60
Lemon Herb Air-Fried Avocado Fries 60
Balsamic Glazed Air-Fried Brussels Sprouts with Cranberries 60

Chapter 11: Sweet Snacks and Desserts 61

Cinnamon Sugar Air-Fried Apple Slices...61
Air-Fried Banana Chips with Cacao Drizzle 61
Almond Flour Air-Fried Donuts with Sugar-Free Glaze 61
Air-Fried Strawberry Shortcake Skewers 61
Chocolate-Dipped Air-Fried Coconut Macaroons 62
Vanilla Cinnamon Air-Fried Pear Slices 62
Air-Fried Pineapple Rings with Honey Lime Drizzle 62
Lemon Poppy Seed Air-Fried Muffins 62
Hazelnut Cocoa Air-Fried Granola Clusters 63
Pumpkin Spice Air-Fried Sweet Potato Chips 63
Air-Fried Blueberry Almond Crisp...63
Honey Caramelized Air-Fried Nectarines 63
Chocolate Hazelnut Stuffed Air-Fried Dates 63
Air-Fried Raspberry Oatmeal Bars 64
Maple Cinnamon Air-Fried Plantain Chips 64
Chai Spiced Air-Fried Pears with Greek Yoghurt 64
Almond Butter Stuffed Air-Fried Apples 64
Coconut Flour Air-Fried Brownies with Walnuts 65
Orange Glazed Air-Fried Peach Slices 65
Peanut Butter Banana Air-Fried Spring Rolls...65

References 66

30-Day Meal Plan 67

Introduction

Welcome to the 'Diabetic Air Fryer Recipe Book,' a culinary journey designed to cater to the tastes and health needs of those managing diabetes. This cookbook is a treasure trove of flavorful, easy-to-follow recipes tailored specifically for individuals seeking delicious meals prepared using the innovative and health-conscious air frying technique.

Living with diabetes requires a thoughtful approach to nutrition without compromising on taste. In these pages, you'll discover a collection of carefully crafted recipes that strike the perfect balance between scrumptious flavours and diabetic-friendly ingredients. From appetisers to main courses, sides, and even delectable desserts, each recipe has been meticulously curated to assist in maintaining stable blood sugar levels while indulging in delightful meals.

The air fryer, known for its ability to create crispy textures with minimal oil, serves as the culinary cornerstone of this book. Embracing this modern kitchen appliance's versatility, these recipes offer a diverse range of options, ensuring that individuals managing diabetes can relish diverse flavours without sacrificing health.

Whether you're new to air frying or a seasoned pro, this book is your go-to resource for creating wholesome, diabetes-friendly meals that don't compromise on taste or satisfaction. Let's embark on a flavorful journey together, where health and culinary delight harmoniously meet on every page.

Chapter 1: Managing Diabetes

Understanding the intricacies of managing diabetes is the cornerstone of a healthier, more balanced lifestyle. In this chapter, we delve into the fundamentals of diabetes management, offering insightful guidance and practical tips to empower individuals in their journey towards better health.

From decoding the nuances of blood sugar control to exploring the significance of a well-rounded diet and the role of physical activity, this chapter serves as a comprehensive guide. We navigate through essential information, providing a clear roadmap for effectively managing diabetes.

Armed with the knowledge and strategies presented in this chapter, individuals can gain a deeper understanding of their condition and embrace proactive approaches to live a fulfilling life while effectively managing diabetes.

What is Diabetes?

Diabetes is a chronic health condition characterised by elevated levels of sugar (glucose) in the blood. This metabolic disorder occurs due to either insufficient production of insulin, the hormone responsible for regulating blood sugar, or the body's inability to effectively use the insulin it produces.

There are primarily three main types of diabetes:

- **1. Type 1 Diabetes:** This results from the immune system mistakenly attacking and destroying insulin-producing cells in the pancreas. Consequently, individuals with Type 1 diabetes require insulin injections to manage their blood sugar levels.
- **2. Type 2 Diabetes:** This type develops when the body becomes resistant to insulin or doesn't produce enough insulin to meet its needs. It is often associated with lifestyle factors like poor diet, sedentary habits, and obesity. Type 2 diabetes can sometimes be managed through lifestyle changes, medication, and, in some cases, insulin therapy.
- **3. Gestational Diabetes:** This form of diabetes occurs during pregnancy when the body cannot produce enough insulin to meet the increased demands. It usually resolves after childbirth but necessitates careful monitoring during pregnancy to prevent complications for both the mother and the baby.

High blood sugar levels associated with diabetes, if left unmanaged, can lead to various complications affecting the heart, kidneys, eyes, nerves, and other vital organs. However, with proper management, including a healthy diet, regular physical activity, medication adherence (if prescribed), and routine monitoring of blood sugar levels, individuals with diabetes can effectively control their condition and minimise the risk of complications.

It's crucial to work closely with healthcare professionals to develop personalised management plans tailored to individual needs, fostering a proactive approach towards achieving optimal health while living with diabetes.

Food To Eat with Diabetes

Nutrition plays a pivotal role in managing diabetes, and making mindful food choices is essential for

maintaining stable blood sugar levels. Here's a guide to the types of foods that can be beneficial for individuals managing diabetes:
- **Complex Carbohydrates:** Opt for whole grains like brown rice, quinoa, whole wheat pasta, and oats. These complex carbohydrates digest more slowly, preventing rapid spikes in blood sugar levels.
- **Non-Starchy Vegetables:** Load up on nutrient-dense vegetables such as leafy greens, broccoli, cauliflower, peppers, and tomatoes. These veggies are low in carbohydrates and calories while being rich in vitamins, minerals, and fibre.
- **Lean Proteins:** Incorporate lean protein sources such as poultry, fish, tofu, legumes, and eggs into your meals. Protein helps maintain satiety and can prevent drastic fluctuations in blood sugar levels.
- **Healthy Fats:** Choose sources of healthy fats like avocados, nuts, seeds, and olive oil. These fats aid in managing cholesterol levels and contribute to overall heart health.
- **Fruits in Moderation:** While fruits contain natural sugars, they also provide essential vitamins and fibre. Opt for lower-sugar fruits like berries, apples, citrus fruits, and melons. Portion control is key due to their natural sugar content.
- **Low-Fat Dairy or Dairy Alternatives:** Select low-fat or fat-free dairy products like yoghurt, milk, and cheese. Alternatively, choose dairy alternatives fortified with calcium and vitamin D, such as almond or soy milk.

Being mindful of portion sizes and the balance of macronutrients (carbohydrates, proteins, and fats) in each meal is not just a strategy, it's a reassurance. Knowing that you're focusing on whole, minimally processed foods can give you confidence in your blood sugar management.

Remember, you're not alone in this journey. Consulting with a registered dietitian or healthcare provider can provide personalised guidance, creating a balanced meal plan that meets your dietary needs and supports optimal diabetes management.

Food To Avoid with Diabetes

Understanding which foods to avoid or limit is crucial in managing blood sugar levels and overall health for individuals with diabetes. Here's a guide outlining foods that are typically recommended to be avoided or consumed in moderation:
- **Sugary Foods and Beverages:** High-sugar items like candies, pastries, cakes, sugary cereals, soda, fruit juices, and sweetened beverages can cause rapid spikes in blood sugar levels. Limiting these items helps maintain stable blood sugar levels.
- **Refined Carbohydrates:** Foods made with refined grains and white flour, such as white bread, white rice, and regular pasta, lack fibre and can lead to quick increases in blood sugar levels. Opt for whole grains whenever possible.
- **Saturated and Trans Fats:** Foods high in unhealthy fats, such as fried foods, fatty cuts of meat, processed snacks, and commercially baked goods, can contribute to heart issues, which individuals with diabetes are more prone to developing.
- **High-Sodium Foods:** Processed and packaged foods, canned soups, and certain condiments often contain high amounts of sodium. Excessive sodium intake may increase the risk of heart disease, which is a concern for people with diabetes.

- **Excessive Alcohol:** Drinking alcohol can affect blood sugar levels and interfere with medication for diabetes. It's essential to consume alcohol in moderation, following healthcare provider recommendations.
- **High-Glycemic Index Foods:** Foods that quickly raise blood sugar levels, such as instant rice, mashed potatoes, and certain breakfast cereals, should be limited. These foods can cause rapid spikes in blood glucose levels.
- **Sweetened Condiments and Sauces:** Condiments like ketchup, barbecue sauce, and sweetened salad dressings often contain added sugars, contributing to increased carbohydrate intake.

While it's crucial to be aware of these food choices, moderation is key. For instance, portion control could mean having a small piece of cake instead of a large one, or having half a cup of mashed potatoes instead of a full cup. Mindful eating habits, such as eating slowly and savouring each bite, also play a significant role in managing diabetes. Individual tolerance to certain foods may vary, so monitoring blood sugar levels after meals can help identify which foods may affect personal glucose levels.

Consulting with a registered dietitian or healthcare provider for personalised dietary recommendations tailored to specific health needs and preferences is highly recommended for effective diabetes management.

Is an Air Fryer Good for Diabetics?

- An air fryer can be a beneficial kitchen tool for individuals managing diabetes due to its ability to prepare healthy meals with reduced oil content. Here are several reasons why an air fryer can be **advantageous for those with diabetes:**
- **Reduced Oil Usage:** Air fryers use hot air circulation to cook food, requiring significantly less oil than traditional frying methods. This reduction in oil helps in controlling overall fat intake, especially saturated and trans fats, which can impact heart health and insulin sensitivity.
- **Healthier Cooking Method:** Air frying minimises the need for deep frying, which can lead to the formation of harmful compounds known as AGEs (Advanced Glycation End Products) when oils are heated to high temperatures. AGEs have been linked to inflammation and complications related to diabetes.
- **Retained Nutritional Value:** The cooking process in an air fryer retains more nutrients compared to deep frying. It helps preserve the natural goodness of foods like vegetables, which are essential for a balanced and nutrient-rich diet.
- **Versatility in Meal Preparation:** Air fryers are versatile appliances that can cook a wide range of foods, from vegetables and proteins to snacks and even desserts. This versatility allows for diverse meal options, enabling individuals to explore various diabetic-friendly recipes.

Control Over Ingredients: Using an air fryer gives greater control over ingredients, allowing individuals to choose healthier options and customise recipes to suit their dietary needs. This control is particularly beneficial for individuals managing diabetes, as it supports adherence to a balanced meal plan.

Remember, an air fryer is a tool, not a magic wand. While it can help make your meals healthier, the ingredients you choose and the balance of your diet are just as important. Whole, unprocessed ingredients and a balanced diet tailored to your needs are key to making the most of your air fryer. Ultimately, incorporating an air fryer into a diabetic meal plan can be a valuable addition, promoting healthier cooking practices and facilitating the preparation of delicious, diabetes-friendly meals with reduced oil content.

Chapter 2: Why Choose Air Fryers?

In this chapter, we embark on an exploration of the remarkable world of air fryers and uncover the compelling reasons behind their rising popularity as a kitchen essential, especially for individuals seeking healthier cooking methods, including those managing diabetes.

Air fryers have revolutionised the culinary landscape by offering a healthier alternative to traditional frying methods. Through the ingenious use of hot air circulation, these compact appliances crisp up food with a fraction of the oil used in conventional frying, presenting a multitude of advantages that cater to various dietary needs.

This chapter delves into the myriad benefits of air fryers, shedding light on why they have become a favoured kitchen companion. From their ability to produce crispy textures while significantly reducing unhealthy fats to their versatility in preparing a wide array of dishes, air fryers offer a gateway to flavourful, yet health-conscious cooking.

How Does an Air Fryer Work

Air fryers, using hot air circulation and convection technology, offer a healthier alternative to traditional frying methods. With adjustable temperature controls and drip trays, they provide versatility and reduced oil usage, beneficial for individuals managing their health, including those with diabetes.

An air fryer operates on a simple yet effective principle, utilising rapid air circulation to cook food evenly and create a crispy exterior, akin to traditional frying but with significantly less oil. Here's a breakdown of how an air fryer works:

- **Hot Air Circulation:** The core mechanism of an air fryer involves a heating element placed above the cooking chamber. This element rapidly heats the air within the appliance, creating intense heat.
- **Convection Technology:** Once the air reaches the desired temperature, a powerful fan inside the air fryer swiftly circulates this hot air around the food placed in a cooking basket or tray. The fan distributes the heat evenly, ensuring that every part of the food receives an equal amount of heat.
- **Maillard Reaction:** As the hot air envelops the food, it triggers the Maillard reaction, a chemical reaction between amino acids and reducing sugars present in the food. This reaction is responsible for browning and creating a crispy texture on the outer surface of the food, similar to the results achieved through frying.
- **Reduced Oil Usage:** Unlike deep frying, which submerges food in oil, air fryers require only a minimal amount of oil, typically a light coating applied directly to the food's surface. This small quantity of oil helps in achieving the desired crispiness while significantly reducing overall fat content.
- **Cooking Variability:** Air fryers often come equipped with adjustable temperature controls and cooking timers, allowing for versatility in preparing various dishes. This flexibility enables

users to set specific temperatures and cooking times tailored to different foods, ensuring optimal results.
- **Drip Tray:** Many air fryers come with a drip tray or basket that collects excess fat or oil released from the food during the cooking process. This design feature contributes to healthier meal preparation by reducing the consumption of excess fats.

In summary, an air fryer's innovative cooking technique relies on hot air circulation, convection technology, and controlled temperatures to create crispy and flavourful dishes with a fraction of the oil typically used in traditional frying methods. This method not only yields appealing textures but also promotes healthier cooking practices, making it an attractive option for individuals seeking to manage their health, including those with diabetes.

The Benefits of Air Frying for Diabetics

Air frying presents many advantages for individuals managing diabetes, offering a convenient and health-conscious cooking method that aligns well with dietary guidelines for blood sugar management. Here are the key benefits of air frying for those with diabetes:
- **Reduced Oil Usage:** Air fryers require significantly less oil compared to traditional frying methods. This reduction in oil intake can be particularly beneficial for individuals with diabetes, as it helps in controlling overall fat consumption and caloric intake, supporting weight management and insulin sensitivity.
- **Healthier Cooking Technique:** Air frying eliminates the need for deep frying, thereby minimising the formation of harmful compounds such as Advanced Glycation End Products (AGEs) that can result from high-temperature cooking with oil. By using hot air circulation, air frying helps retain the nutritional integrity of foods without compromising on taste or texture.
- **Control Over Ingredients:** Using an air fryer allows for greater control over the ingredients used in cooking. Individuals managing diabetes can choose healthier oil options or opt for minimal oil altogether, ensuring a more conscious selection of ingredients to suit their dietary needs.
- **Retained Nutritional Value:** Air frying preserves the natural goodness of foods, including vegetables and lean proteins, by cooking them quickly at high temperatures. This method helps retain essential nutrients, vitamins, and minerals, supporting a well-rounded and balanced diet crucial for individuals with diabetes.
- **Versatility in Meal Preparation:** Air fryers offer versatility in preparing a wide range of dishes, from crispy vegetables to lean meats and even desserts. This flexibility allows individuals to experiment with various diabetic-friendly recipes, ensuring a diverse and enjoyable meal plan.
- **Easy Cleanup:** Air fryers often come with non-stick cooking baskets or trays that are easy to clean. This convenience not only saves time but also encourages consistent and healthy cooking practices.

By harnessing the benefits of air frying, individuals managing diabetes can enjoy flavorful meals without compromising on health. Incorporating an air fryer into their cooking routine can contribute to a more balanced and diabetes-friendly diet, promoting better blood sugar management and overall well-being.

How to Clean and Maintain Your Air Fryer

Proper maintenance and regular cleaning are essential to ensure your air fryer's longevity and optimal performance. Here's a step-by-step guide on how to clean and maintain your air fryer:
1. Read the Manual: Familiarise yourself with the

manufacturer's instructions and recommendations for cleaning and maintenance specific to your air fryer model. This step ensures you follow the correct procedures without damaging any components.

2. Unplug and Cool Down: Always unplug the air fryer and allow it to cool down completely before starting the cleaning process. This prevents the risk of burns or electric shock.

3. Detach Removable Parts: Most air fryers come with removable parts such as the cooking basket, tray, and pan. Remove these parts carefully and wash them with warm, soapy water. Use a non-abrasive sponge or cloth to avoid scratching the surfaces.

4. Clean the Interior: Wipe the interior of the air fryer with a damp cloth or sponge to remove any food residue or grease. Be cautious around the heating element to prevent damage.

5. Address Stubborn Residue: For stubborn stains or food particles, soak the removable parts in warm, soapy water for some time to loosen the debris. Use a soft-bristled brush or sponge to gently scrub away the residue.

6. Dry Thoroughly: After washing, ensure all components are completely dry before reassembling the air fryer. Moisture can lead to mould growth or electrical issues, so thorough drying is crucial.

7. Clean the Exterior: Wipe the exterior of the air fryer with a damp cloth to remove any spills or stains. Avoid using abrasive cleaners or harsh chemicals that could damage the finish.

8. Maintain Regularly: Establish a routine for cleaning your air fryer after each use to prevent the buildup of grease or food residue. Regular maintenance will keep your appliance in top condition.

9. Check for Wear and Tear: Periodically inspect the components for any signs of wear or damage. Replace any worn-out parts following the manufacturer's recommendations to ensure safe operation.

10. Store Properly: Store the air fryer in a dry and clean place when not in use, ensuring proper ventilation to prevent moisture buildup.

By following these cleaning and maintenance practices, you can keep your air fryer in excellent condition, prolong its lifespan, and continue enjoying healthy and delicious meals.

Tips and Tricks for Using Air Fryers

Maximising the potential of your air fryer involves understanding its capabilities and implementing some helpful tips and tricks. Here's a comprehensive guide to making the most out of your air frying experience:

1. Preheat the Air Fryer: Preheating your air fryer for a few minutes before adding the food can enhance cooking results by ensuring even heat distribution and faster cooking times.

2. Use a Light Coating of Oil: While air fryers require less oil than traditional frying methods, a light mist or brushing of oil on food items can promote crispiness and enhance flavours without excess fat.

3. Avoid Overcrowding: To achieve a crispy texture, ensure there's ample space between food items in the air fryer basket. Overcrowding can hinder proper air circulation, resulting in unevenly cooked food.

4. Shake or Flip the Food: To ensure even cooking, shake or flip the food halfway through the cooking time. This simple step helps achieve uniform browning and crispiness on all sides.

5. Experiment with Different Foods: Air fryers are versatile and can cook various foods, from vegetables and meats to frozen items and even baked goods. Experiment with different recipes and foods to explore the appliance's capabilities.

6. Use Parchment Paper or Basket Liners: Line the bottom of the air fryer basket with parchment paper or specially designed basket liners to prevent food from sticking. This makes cleanup easier and protects the basket from scratches.

7. Keep an Eye on Cooking Times: Adjust cooking

times based on the specific food being prepared. Thinner or smaller items may cook faster, so monitoring cooking progress is essential to prevent overcooking.

8. Season Food Before Cooking: Seasoning food before placing it in the air fryer can enhance flavours. Use herbs, spices, marinades, or rubs to add zest to your dishes.

9. Make Use of Accessories: Some air fryers come with additional accessories like racks, skewers, or baking pans. Utilise these accessories to expand your cooking options and prepare a wider variety of meals.

10. Clean Regularly and Follow Manufacturer Guidelines: Proper maintenance is crucial for optimal performance. Clean your air fryer after each use as per the manufacturer's instructions to ensure longevity and safe operation.

By incorporating these tips and tricks into your air frying routine, you can elevate your culinary creations, enjoy healthier meals, and make the most of this versatile kitchen appliance.

FAQs

Curiosity often surrounds the realm of air fryers, from their functionality to their suitability for various foods and dietary needs. This section aims to address common questions individuals might have about air fryers, shedding light on their usage, benefits, maintenance, and their potential role in specific diets, such as managing diabetes.

What defines an air fryer, and how does it operate?
An air fryer is a kitchen appliance designed to cook food by circulating hot air. Using convection technology, it distributes heat evenly, resulting in a crispy outer layer while using minimal oil.

Are air fryers a healthier choice compared to traditional frying methods?
Yes, air fryers use significantly less oil, reducing the fat content in cooked foods and offering a healthier alternative to traditional frying.

Is it possible to cook different foods simultaneously in an air fryer?
While possible, it's essential to consider cooking times and temperatures. Ensure similar cooking requirements for various foods to achieve even results.

Should I preheat an air fryer before use?
Preheating the air fryer for a few minutes is advisable for improved cooking outcomes, ensuring even cooking and desired crispiness.

Can accessories like aluminium foil be used in the air fryer?
Yes, aluminium foil can line the basket or wrap food, but it's crucial to ensure it doesn't hinder air circulation. Many air fryers also offer compatible accessories for diverse cooking needs.

What's the recommended way to clean an air fryer?
Cleaning involves washing removable parts with warm, soapy water and wiping the interior and exterior. Refer to the manufacturer's instructions for specific cleaning guidance.

Can frozen foods be cooked directly in the air fryer?
Yes, air fryers excel at cooking frozen items like fries or nuggets. Adjust cooking times per package instructions or until achieving the desired crispness.

Are there foods unsuitable for air frying?
While versatile, foods with excessive breading or delicate textures may pose challenges. Careful consideration is necessary for optimal results.

Is it safe to leave the air fryer unattended during cooking?
While generally safe, periodic monitoring is recommended, especially when trying new recipes or food items.

Can air fryers assist in managing a diabetic diet?
Air fryers, with their reduced oil usage, can aid in preparing diabetes-friendly meals focused on balanced nutrition and reduced fat content.

These FAQs aim to provide clarity on common queries about air fryers, addressing their usage, maintenance, and their potential role in catering to various dietary needs.

Chapter 3: Breakfast Recipes

Air Fryer Veggie Omelette

Serves: 2
Prep time: 10 minutes / Cook time: 12 minutes

Ingredients:
- 4 large eggs
- 60ml whole milk
- 40g red pepper, diced
- 40g green pepper, diced
- 40g onion, finely chopped
- 40g mushrooms, sliced
- 30g spinach, chopped
- 30g shredded cheddar cheese
- Salt and black pepper, to taste
- Cooking spray or a little oil for greasing

Preparation instructions:
1. Preheat the Air Fryer to 180°C for 5 minutes.
2. In a bowl, whisk together eggs, whole milk, salt, and black pepper until well combined.
3. Grease the air fryer-safe pan or dish with cooking spray or a little oil.
4. Spread the diced bell peppers, onions, mushrooms, and chopped spinach evenly in the greased pan.
5. Pour the egg mixture over the vegetables in the pan. Sprinkle shredded cheddar cheese on top.
6. Place the pan in the air fryer basket and cook at 180°C for 12 minutes or until the omelette is set and slightly golden on the edges.
7. Once done, carefully remove the omelette from the air fryer. Let it cool for a minute before slicing and serving.

Crispy Turkey Bacon

Serves: 4
Prep time: 5 minutes / Cook time: 10 minutes

Ingredients:
- 8 slices turkey bacon

Preparation instructions:
1. Preheat the Air Fryer to 200°C for 3 minutes.
2. Place the turkey bacon slices in a single layer in the air fryer basket.
3. Air fry at 200°C for 8-10 minutes, flipping the bacon halfway through the cooking time.
4. Cook until the bacon reaches the desired crispiness.
5. Remove the crispy turkey bacon from the air fryer and place it on a paper towel-lined plate to absorb excess grease.
6. Serve hot as a side or use in your favourite breakfast dishes.

Low-Carb Breakfast Burritos

Serves: 4
Prep time: 15 minutes / Cook time: 12 minutes

Ingredients:
- 8 large eggs
- 60ml heavy cream
- 200g turkey or pork sausage, cooked and crumbled
- 100g shredded cheddar cheese
- 40g green bell pepper, diced
- 40g onion, finely chopped
- 4 low-carb tortillas
- Salt and black pepper, to taste
- Cooking spray or a little oil for greasing

Preparation instructions:
1. Preheat the Air Fryer to 180°C for 5 minutes.
2. In a bowl, whisk together eggs, heavy cream, salt, and black pepper until well combined.
3. Grease the air fryer-safe pan or dish with cooking spray or a little oil.
4. Spread the diced bell peppers and onions evenly in the greased pan.
5. Pour the egg mixture over the vegetables in the pan. Sprinkle crumbled sausage and shredded cheddar cheese on top.
6. Place the pan in the air fryer basket and cook at 180°C for 12 minutes or until the eggs are set.
7. Warm the low-carb tortillas in the air fryer for 1-2 minutes.
8. Once done, spoon the cooked egg mixture onto the warmed tortillas, fold, and roll to make burritos.
9. Serve the low-carb breakfast burritos warm and enjoy!

Air-Fried Avocado and Egg

Serves: 2
Prep time: 10 minutes / Cook time: 8 minutes

Ingredients:
- 2 ripe avocados
- 2 large eggs
- 15ml olive oil
- Salt and black pepper, to taste
- Chopped fresh herbs (optional), for garnish

Preparation instructions:
1. Preheat the Air Fryer to 180°C for 5 minutes.
2. Cut the avocados in half and remove the pits.
3. Scoop out a little extra avocado flesh from each half to create a larger hollow space for the egg.
4. Brush the avocado halves with olive oil and season with salt and black pepper.
5. Carefully crack an egg into each avocado half, placing it in the hollowed-out space.
6. Place the avocado halves in the air fryer basket.
7. Air fry at 180°C for 8 minutes or until the eggs reach your desired level of doneness.
8. Once done, carefully remove the avocado and egg from the air fryer.
9. Garnish with chopped fresh herbs if desired, and serve warm.

Cinnamon Apple Chips

Serves: 4
Prep time: 10 minutes / Cook time: 12 minutes

Ingredients:
- 2 medium apples
- 5g ground cinnamon
- Cooking spray

Preparation instructions:
1. Preheat the Air Fryer to 120°C for 5 minutes.
2. Wash the apples thoroughly and slice them thinly using a sharp knife or a mandoline slicer.
3. In a bowl, toss the apple slices with ground cinnamon until evenly coated.
4. Lightly grease the air fryer basket with cooking spray.
5. Place the apple slices in a single layer in the air fryer basket, ensuring they do not overlap.
6. Air fry at 120°C for 12 minutes, flipping the slices halfway through the cooking time.
7. Check for desired crispiness; if needed, continue air frying for an additional 1-2 minutes.
8. Once crispy and golden, remove the cinnamon apple chips from the air fryer.
9. Let them cool completely before serving for optimal crispiness.

Sweet Potato Hash Browns

Serves: 4
Prep time: 15 minutes / Cook time: 15 minutes

Ingredients:
- 500g sweet potatoes, peeled and grated
- 30g onion, finely chopped
- 30g cornstarch
- 30ml olive oil
- 1/2 tsp paprika
- Salt and black pepper, to taste

Preparation instructions:
1. Preheat the Air Fryer to 200°C for 5 minutes.
2. Place the grated sweet potatoes in a clean kitchen towel and squeeze out excess moisture.
3. In a bowl, combine the grated sweet potatoes, finely chopped onion, cornstarch, olive oil, paprika, salt, and black pepper. Mix until well combined.
4. Divide the mixture into 8 equal portions and shape each portion into a patty.
5. Lightly grease the air fryer basket with cooking spray or a little oil.
6. Place the sweet potato patties in the air fryer basket in a single layer.
7. Air fry at 200°C for 15 minutes, flipping the patties halfway through the cooking time.
8. Once crispy and golden brown, remove the sweet potato hash browns from the air fryer.
9. Serve hot as a delicious side dish or breakfast option.

Low-Carb French Toast Sticks

Serves: 4
Prep time: 10 minutes / Cook time: 10 minutes

Ingredients:
- 4 slices low-carb bread (approximately 120g)
- 2 large eggs
- 60ml unsweetened almond milk
- 1/2 tsp vanilla extract
- 1/2 tsp ground cinnamon

- Cooking spray or a little oil for greasing

Preparation instructions:
1. Preheat the Air Fryer to 180°C for 5 minutes.
2. Cut each slice of low-carb bread into sticks or fingers.
3. In a shallow bowl, whisk together eggs, almond milk, vanilla extract, and ground cinnamon until well combined.
4. Dip each breadstick into the egg mixture, ensuring it's evenly coated.
5. Lightly grease the air fryer basket with cooking spray or a little oil.
6. Place the coated bread sticks in a single layer in the air fryer basket, leaving space between them.
7. Air fry at 180°C for 10 minutes, flipping the sticks halfway through the cooking time.
8. Once crispy and golden, remove the low-carb French toast sticks from the air fryer.
9. Serve warm with your choice of low-carb syrup or fresh berries.

Zucchini Fritters

Serves: 4
Prep time: 15 minutes / Cook time: 10 minutes

Ingredients:
- 2 medium zucchinis (approximately 400g), grated and excess moisture squeezed out
- 1 egg
- 30g grated Parmesan cheese
- 30g almond flour
- 2 cloves garlic, minced
- 1/4 tsp dried oregano
- Salt and black pepper, to taste
- Cooking spray or a little oil for greasing

Preparation instructions:
1. Preheat the Air Fryer to 200°C for 5 minutes.
2. In a bowl, combine grated zucchini, egg, grated Parmesan cheese, almond flour, minced garlic, dried oregano, salt, and black pepper. Mix well.
3. Form the mixture into small patties or fritters.
4. Lightly grease the air fryer basket with cooking spray or a little oil.
5. Place the zucchini fritters in the air fryer basket in a single layer.
6. Air fry at 200°C for 10 minutes, flipping the fritters halfway through the cooking time.
7. Once crispy and golden, remove the zucchini fritters from the air fryer.
8. Serve hot as a delightful breakfast side or light meal option.

Air Fryer Breakfast Sausages

Serves: 4
Prep time: 5 minutes / Cook time: 10 minutes

Ingredients:
- 8 breakfast sausages (approximately 400g)

Preparation instructions:
1. Preheat the Air Fryer to 180°C for 5 minutes.
2. Place the breakfast sausages in the air fryer basket in a single layer.
3. Air fry at 180°C for 10 minutes, turning the sausages halfway through the cooking time.
4. Ensure the sausages are cooked through and reach an internal temperature of 75°C.
5. Once done, remove the breakfast sausages from the air fryer.
6. Serve hot as a classic breakfast item or use in your favourite breakfast recipes.

Spinach and Feta Egg Muffins

Serves: 4
Prep time: 10 minutes / Cook time: 15 minutes

Ingredients:
- 6 large eggs
- 60ml whole milk
- 60g fresh spinach, chopped
- 50g feta cheese, crumbled
- Salt and black pepper, to taste
- Cooking spray or a little oil for greasing

Preparation instructions:
1. Preheat the Air Fryer to 180°C for 5 minutes.
2. In a bowl, whisk together eggs, whole milk, salt, and black pepper until well combined.
3. Add the chopped fresh spinach and crumbled feta cheese to the egg mixture. Mix gently.
4. Lightly grease the silicone muffin cups or an air fryer-safe pan with cooking spray or a little oil.
5. Pour the egg mixture evenly into 4 silicone muffin cups or the prepared pan.
6. Place the muffin cups or pan in the air fryer

basket.
7. Air fry at 180°C for 15 minutes or until the egg muffins are set and slightly golden on top.
8. Once done, remove the spinach and feta egg muffins from the air fryer.
9. Let them cool for a minute before serving.

Cauliflower Hash Browns

Serves: 4
Prep time: 15 minutes / Cook time: 20 minutes

Ingredients:
- 400g cauliflower florets, steamed and grated
- 1 large egg
- 30g almond flour
- 30g grated Parmesan cheese
- 1/2 tsp garlic powder
- 1/2 tsp onion powder
- Salt and black pepper, to taste
- Cooking spray or a little oil for greasing

Preparation instructions:
1. Preheat the Air Fryer to 200°C for 5 minutes.
2. In a bowl, combine grated cauliflower, egg, almond flour, grated Parmesan cheese, garlic powder, onion powder, salt, and black pepper. Mix well.
3. Form the cauliflower mixture into small patties or hash browns.
4. Lightly grease the air fryer basket with cooking spray or a little oil.
5. Place the cauliflower hash browns in the air fryer basket in a single layer.
6. Air fry at 200°C for 20 minutes, flipping the hash browns halfway through the cooking time.
7. Once crispy and golden brown, remove the cauliflower hash browns from the air fryer.
8. Serve hot as a nutritious breakfast option.

Crispy Tofu Scramble

Serves: 4
Prep time: 10 minutes / Cook time: 15 minutes

Ingredients:
- 400g firm tofu, drained and crumbled
- 30ml olive oil
- 1/2 tsp turmeric powder
- 1/2 tsp paprika
- 1/4 tsp garlic powder
- 1/4 tsp onion powder
- Salt and black pepper, to taste
- Chopped fresh parsley (optional), for garnish

Preparation instructions:
1. Preheat the Air Fryer to 180°C for 5 minutes.
2. In a bowl, toss crumbled tofu with olive oil, turmeric powder, paprika, garlic powder, onion powder, salt, and black pepper until well coated.
3. Spread the seasoned tofu in the air fryer basket in a single layer.
4. Air fry at 180°C for 15 minutes, shaking the basket or stirring the tofu halfway through the cooking time.
5. Once the tofu is crispy and lightly browned, remove it from the air fryer.
6. Garnish with chopped fresh parsley if desired, and serve the crispy tofu scramble hot.

Almond Flour Pancakes

Serves: 4
Prep time: 10 minutes / Cook time: 10 minutes

Ingredients:
- 120g almond flour
- 2 large eggs
- 60ml unsweetened almond milk
- 2 tbsp erythritol (or preferred sweetener)
- 1 tsp baking powder
- 1/2 tsp vanilla extract
- Cooking spray or a little oil for greasing

Preparation instructions:
1. Preheat the Air Fryer to 180°C for 5 minutes.
2. In a bowl, whisk together almond flour, eggs, almond milk, erythritol, baking powder, and vanilla extract until a smooth batter forms.
3. Lightly grease the air fryer pan or tray with cooking spray or a little oil.
4. Pour 1/4 cup of batter onto the air fryer pan for each pancake, leaving space between them.
5. Air fry at 180°C for 5 minutes.
6. After 5 minutes, carefully flip the pancakes using a spatula.
7. Air fry for an additional 5 minutes or until the pancakes are golden brown and cooked through.
8. Remove the almond flour pancakes from the

air fryer and serve warm with your favourite toppings.

Low-Carb Sausage Balls

Serves: 4
Prep time: 10 minutes / Cook time: 12 minutes

Ingredients:
- 400g pork sausage meat
- 50g almond flour
- 50g shredded cheddar cheese
- 1/2 tsp baking powder
- 1/4 tsp garlic powder
- 1/4 tsp onion powder
- Salt and black pepper, to taste
- Cooking spray or a little oil for greasing

Preparation instructions:
1. Preheat the Air Fryer to 180°C for 5 minutes.
2. In a bowl, combine pork sausage meat, almond flour, shredded cheddar cheese, baking powder, garlic powder, onion powder, salt, and black pepper. Mix until well combined.
3. Form the mixture into small balls, about 1 tablespoon each.
4. Lightly grease the air fryer basket with cooking spray or a little oil.
5. Place the sausage balls in the air fryer basket in a single layer.
6. Air fry at 180°C for 12 minutes, turning the balls halfway through the cooking time.
7. Once the sausage balls are cooked through and golden brown, remove them from the air fryer.
8. Serve hot as a delicious low-carb breakfast option or snack.

Egg and Veggie Breakfast Wraps

Serves: 4
Prep time: 15 minutes / Cook time: 10 minutes

Ingredients:
- 4 large eggs
- 60ml unsweetened almond milk
- 60g bell peppers, diced
- 60g mushrooms, sliced
- 40g onion, finely chopped
- 40g spinach, chopped
- 30g shredded cheddar cheese
- Salt and black pepper, to taste
- Cooking spray or a little oil for greasing
- 4 low-carb tortillas

Preparation instructions:
1. Preheat the Air Fryer to 180°C for 5 minutes.
2. In a bowl, whisk together eggs, almond milk, salt, and black pepper until well combined.
3. In a separate pan, sauté diced bell peppers, sliced mushrooms, chopped onion, and chopped spinach until softened.
4. Grease the air fryer-safe pan or dish with cooking spray or a little oil.
5. Pour the whisked egg mixture into the greased pan.
6. Add the sautéed vegetables and shredded cheddar cheese on top of the egg mixture.
7. Place the pan in the air fryer basket.
8. Air fry at 180°C for 10 minutes or until the eggs are set.
9. Warm the low-carb tortillas in the air fryer for 1-2 minutes.
10. Once done, spoon the cooked egg and veggie mixture onto the warmed tortillas.
11. Roll the tortillas to form wraps and serve these delightful egg and veggie breakfast wraps.

Air-Fried Breakfast Quinoa

Serves: 4
Prep time: 10 minutes / Cook time: 20 minutes

Ingredients:
- 200g quinoa, cooked and cooled
- 60g diced bell peppers
- 60g diced tomatoes
- 40g diced onions
- 40g chopped spinach
- 4 large eggs
- 30g grated Parmesan cheese
- 15ml olive oil
- 1/2 tsp paprika
- Salt and black pepper, to taste

Preparation instructions:
1. Preheat the Air Fryer to 180°C for 5 minutes.
2. In a bowl, mix together cooked quinoa, diced bell peppers, diced tomatoes, diced onions, chopped spinach, olive oil, paprika, salt, and black pepper.
3. Divide the quinoa mixture into 4 sections in the

air fryer-safe pan or dish.
4. Create a well in the centre of each quinoa section and crack an egg into each well.
5. Sprinkle grated Parmesan cheese over the quinoa and eggs.
6. Air fry at 180°C for 15-20 minutes or until the egg whites are set and the yolks reach your desired consistency.
7. Once cooked, remove the air-fried breakfast quinoa from the air fryer and serve warm.

Turkey and Egg Breakfast Cups

Serves: 4
Prep time: 10 minutes / Cook time: 15 minutes

Ingredients:
- 8 slices turkey bacon
- 4 large eggs
- 60g shredded mozzarella cheese
- 30g diced bell peppers
- 30g diced onions
- 15g chopped parsley
- Salt and black pepper, to taste
- Cooking spray or a little oil for greasing

Preparation instructions:
1. Preheat the Air Fryer to 180°C for 5 minutes.
2. Line 4 silicone muffin cups with turkey bacon slices to create cups.
3. Crack an egg into each turkey bacon cup.
4. Top each egg with shredded mozzarella cheese, diced bell peppers, diced onions, chopped parsley, salt, and black pepper.
5. Lightly grease the air fryer basket with cooking spray or a little oil.
6. Place the filled muffin cups in the air fryer basket.
7. Air fry at 180°C for 12-15 minutes or until the egg whites are set and the bacon is crispy.
8. Once done, remove the turkey and egg breakfast cups from the air fryer and let them cool for a minute before serving.

Low-Carb Cheese and Bacon Biscuits

Serves: 4
Prep time: 15 minutes / Cook time: 10 minutes

Ingredients:
- 100g almond flour
- 50g shredded cheddar cheese
- 50g cooked bacon, crumbled
- 2 large eggs
- 30ml heavy cream
- 1/2 tsp baking powder
- 1/4 tsp garlic powder
- Salt and black pepper, to taste

Preparation instructions:
1. Preheat the Air Fryer to 180°C for 5 minutes.
2. In a bowl, mix almond flour, shredded cheddar cheese, crumbled bacon, baking powder, garlic powder, salt, and black pepper.
3. In a separate bowl, whisk together eggs and heavy cream.
4. Combine the wet and dry ingredients, stirring until well combined.
5. Form the mixture into 4 biscuit-shaped rounds.
6. Lightly grease the air fryer basket with cooking spray or a little oil.
7. Place the biscuit rounds in the air fryer basket.
8. Air fry at 180°C for 8-10 minutes or until the biscuits are golden brown and cooked through.
9. Once cooked, remove the low-carb cheese and bacon biscuits from the air fryer and let them cool slightly before serving.

Crispy Kale Chips

Serves: 4
Prep time: 10 minutes / Cook time: 8 minutes

Ingredients:
- 200g fresh kale leaves, stems removed and torn into bite-sized pieces
- 15ml olive oil
- 1/4 tsp garlic powder
- 1/4 tsp paprika
- Salt, to taste

Preparation instructions:
1. Preheat the Air Fryer to 160°C for 5 minutes.
2. In a bowl, toss the kale leaves with olive oil, garlic powder, paprika, and a pinch of salt until evenly coated.
3. Spread the seasoned kale leaves in the air fryer basket in a single layer.
4. Air fry at 160°C for 6-8 minutes or until the kale is crispy and slightly browned, shaking the basket halfway through the cooking time.
5. Once crispy, remove the kale chips from the air fryer and let them cool before serving.

Breakfast Stuffed Peppers

Serves: 4
Prep time: 15 minutes / Cook time: 20 minutes

Ingredients:
- 4 medium bell peppers
- 8 large eggs
- 120g cooked breakfast sausage, crumbled
- 60g diced tomatoes
- 60g shredded cheddar cheese
- Salt and black pepper, to taste
- Cooking spray or a little oil for greasing

Preparation instructions:
1. Preheat the Air Fryer to 180°C for 5 minutes.
2. Slice off the tops of the bell peppers and remove the seeds and membranes.
3. In a bowl, beat the eggs and season with salt and black pepper.
4. Stir in crumbled breakfast sausage, diced tomatoes, and shredded cheddar cheese into the egg mixture.
5. Lightly grease the air fryer basket with cooking spray or a little oil.
6. Fill each bell pepper with the egg mixture.
7. Place the stuffed peppers in the air fryer basket.
8. Air fry at 180°C for 18-20 minutes or until the peppers are tender and the egg mixture is cooked through.
9. Once cooked, remove the breakfast stuffed peppers from the air fryer and let them cool slightly before serving.

Coconut Flour Waffles

Serves: 4
Prep time: 10 minutes / Cook time: 10 minutes

Ingredients:
- 80g coconut flour
- 4 large eggs
- 240 ml unsweetened almond milk
- 30ml melted coconut oil
- 1 tsp baking powder
- 1 tsp vanilla extract
- Cooking spray or a little oil for greasing

Preparation instructions:
1. Preheat the waffle iron and lightly grease with cooking spray or a little oil.
2. In a bowl, whisk together coconut flour, eggs, almond milk, melted coconut oil, baking powder, and vanilla extract until smooth.
3. Pour the batter onto the waffle iron and cook according to the manufacturer's instructions until golden brown and crispy.
4. Once cooked, carefully remove the coconut flour waffles from the waffle iron and serve warm.

Aubergine and Tomato Breakfast Stack

Serves: 4
Prep time: 15 minutes / Cook time: 20 minutes

Ingredients:
- 400g aubergine, sliced
- 400g tomatoes, sliced
- 100g mozzarella cheese, sliced
- 60ml olive oil
- 2 cloves garlic, minced
- 1 tsp dried basil
- Salt and black pepper, to taste

Preparation instructions:
1. Preheat the Air Fryer to 180°C for 5 minutes.
2. In a bowl, toss aubergine slices with olive oil, minced garlic, dried basil, salt, and black pepper.
3. Place the seasoned aubergine slices in the air fryer basket.
4. Air fry at 180°C for 8-10 minutes on each side or until golden and tender.
5. Once done, remove the aubergine slices from the air fryer and set them aside.
6. In the same air fryer basket, add tomato slices and air fry for 3-5 minutes until slightly softened.
7. Assemble the breakfast stacks by layering eggplant, tomato, and mozzarella cheese slices.
8. Place the stacks back in the air fryer for 3-5 minutes or until the cheese is melted.
9. Once the cheese is melted and bubbly, remove the breakfast stacks from the air fryer and serve warm.

Cottage Cheese Pancakes

Serves: 4
Prep time: 10 minutes / Cook time: 10 minutes

Ingredients:
- 200g cottage cheese
- 4 large eggs
- 60g almond flour
- 30ml unsweetened almond milk
- 1 tsp baking powder
- 1 tsp vanilla extract
- Cooking spray or a little oil for greasing

Preparation instructions:
1. In a blender, combine cottage cheese, eggs, almond flour, almond milk, baking powder, and vanilla extract. Blend until smooth.
2. Preheat the Air Fryer to 180°C for 5 minutes.
3. Lightly grease the air fryer basket with cooking spray or a little oil.
4. Pour the pancake batter onto the air fryer basket in small rounds.
5. Air fry at 180°C for 5 minutes.
6. After 5 minutes, carefully flip the pancakes using a spatula.
7. Air fry for an additional 3-5 minutes or until the pancakes are cooked through and golden brown.
8. Once done, remove the cottage cheese pancakes from the air fryer and serve warm.

Air-Fried Breakfast Potatoes

Serves: 4

Prep time: 15 minutes / Cook time: 25 minutes

Ingredients:
- 600g potatoes, diced
- 30ml olive oil
- 2 tsp paprika
- 1 tsp garlic powder
- 1 tsp onion powder
- Salt and black pepper, to taste

Preparation instructions:
1. Preheat the Air Fryer to 200°C for 5 minutes.
2. In a bowl, toss diced potatoes with olive oil, paprika, garlic powder, onion powder, salt, and black pepper until evenly coated.
3. Spread the seasoned potatoes in the air fryer basket in a single layer.
4. Air fry at 200°C for 20-25 minutes, shaking the basket occasionally, until the potatoes are crispy and cooked through.
5. Once crispy, remove the breakfast potatoes from the air fryer and serve hot.

Low-Carb Breakfast Pizza

Serves: 4

Prep time: 15 minutes / Cook time: 12 minutes

Ingredients:
- 200g almond flour
- 2 large eggs
- 100g shredded mozzarella cheese
- 60g diced peppers
- 60g diced onions
- 60g sliced mushrooms
- 120g sugar-free marinara sauce
- 30g grated Parmesan cheese
- 1 tsp dried oregano
- Salt and black pepper, to taste

Preparation instructions:
1. Preheat the Air Fryer to 180°C for 5 minutes.
2. In a bowl, combine almond flour and eggs to form a dough.
3. Press the dough into the bottom of an air fryer-safe pan or dish, forming a crust.
4. Spread marinara sauce over the crust evenly.
5. Top with shredded mozzarella cheese, diced peppers, diced onions, and sliced mushrooms.
6. Sprinkle dried oregano, grated Parmesan cheese, salt, and black pepper on top.
7. Air fry at 180°C for 10-12 minutes or until the cheese is melted and bubbly and the crust is golden brown.
8. Once cooked, remove the low-carb breakfast pizza from the air fryer and let it cool slightly before slicing and serving.

Chapter 4: Main Recipes

Air-Fried Lemon Herb Chicken Breasts

Serves: 4
Prep time: 15 minutes / Cook time: 20 minutes

Ingredients:
- 4 boneless, skinless chicken breasts (about 600g)
- 30ml olive oil
- 1 lemon (zest and juice)
- 2 cloves garlic, minced
- 2 tsp dried mixed herbs (such as thyme, rosemary, and oregano)
- Salt and black pepper, to taste

Preparation instructions:
1. Preheat the Air Fryer to 180°C for 5 minutes.
2. In a bowl, combine olive oil, lemon zest, lemon juice, minced garlic, dried herbs, salt, and black pepper.
3. Place the chicken breasts in the marinade, ensuring they are coated evenly.
4. Transfer the marinated chicken breasts to the air fryer basket.
5. Air fry at 180°C for 18-20 minutes, flipping halfway through the cooking time, until the chicken reaches an internal temperature of 75°C and the exterior is golden and crispy.
6. Once cooked, remove the lemon herb chicken breasts from the air fryer and let them rest for a few minutes before serving.

Turkey Meatballs with Marinara Sauce

Serves: 4
Prep time: 20 minutes / Cook time: 15 minutes

Ingredients:
- 500g ground turkey
- 30g breadcrumbs
- 1 egg
- 30g grated Parmesan cheese
- 1 tsp dried oregano
- 1/2 tsp garlic powder
- 1/2 tsp onion powder
- Salt and black pepper, to taste
- 480ml marinara sauce

Preparation instructions:
1. Preheat the Air Fryer to 180°C for 5 minutes.
2. In a bowl, combine ground turkey, breadcrumbs, egg, Parmesan cheese, dried oregano, garlic powder, onion powder, salt, and black pepper. Mix until well combined.
3. Shape the mixture into meatballs, approximately 1 inch in diameter.
4. Place the meatballs in the air fryer basket.
5. Air fry at 180°C for 12-15 minutes, shaking the basket occasionally, until the meatballs are cooked through and golden.
6. In a saucepan, warm the marinara sauce.
7. Once the meatballs are done, toss them in the marinara sauce until coated.
8. Serve the turkey meatballs with marinara sauce.

Cajun Seasoned Air-Fried Shrimp

Serves: 4
Prep time: 10 minutes / Cook time: 8 minutes

Ingredients:
- 500g large shrimp, peeled and deveined
- 30ml olive oil
- 2 tsp Cajun seasoning
- 1/2 tsp garlic powder
- 1/2 tsp onion powder
- 1/2 tsp paprika
- Salt and black pepper, to taste
- Lemon wedges, for serving (optional)

Preparation instructions:
1. Preheat the Air Fryer to 200°C for 5 minutes.
2. In a bowl, toss shrimp with olive oil, Cajun seasoning, garlic powder, onion powder, paprika, salt, and black pepper until evenly coated.
3. Place the seasoned shrimp in the air fryer basket.
4. Air fry at 200°C for 6-8 minutes, shaking the basket halfway through the cooking time, until the shrimp are pink and cooked through.
5. Once cooked, remove the Cajun seasoned air-fried shrimp from the air fryer and serve immediately with lemon wedges if desired.

Garlic Parmesan Air-Fried Chicken Wings

Serves: 4
Prep time: 10 minutes / Cook time: 25 minutes

Ingredients:
- 800g chicken wings
- 30g grated Parmesan cheese
- 2 cloves garlic, minced
- 30ml olive oil
- 1 tsp dried parsley
- 1/2 tsp paprika
- Salt and black pepper, to taste

Preparation instructions:
1. Preheat the Air Fryer to 200°C for 5 minutes.
2. In a bowl, toss chicken wings with grated Parmesan cheese, minced garlic, olive oil, dried parsley, paprika, salt, and black pepper until the wings are evenly coated.
3. Place the chicken wings in the air fryer basket.
4. Air fry at 200°C for 20-25 minutes, flipping the wings halfway through the cooking time, until they are crispy and golden brown.
5. Once cooked, remove the garlic Parmesan air-fried chicken wings from the air fryer and let them rest for a couple of minutes before serving.

Herbed Pork Tenderloin Medallions

Serves: 4
Prep time: 15 minutes / Cook time: 15 minutes

Ingredients:
- 600g pork tenderloin, sliced into medallions
- 30ml olive oil
- 2 tsp dried mixed herbs (such as thyme, rosemary, and sage)
- 1/2 tsp garlic powder
- 1/2 tsp onion powder
- Salt and black pepper, to taste

Preparation instructions:
1. Preheat the Air Fryer to 190°C for 5 minutes.
2. In a bowl, coat pork tenderloin medallions with olive oil, dried mixed herbs, garlic powder, onion powder, salt, and black pepper.
3. Place the pork medallions in the air fryer basket.
4. Air fry at 190°C for 12-15 minutes, flipping halfway through the cooking time, until the pork is cooked through and golden brown.
5. Once cooked, remove the herbed pork tenderloin medallions from the air fryer and let them rest for a few minutes before serving.

Teriyaki Glazed Salmon Fillets

Serves: 4
Prep time: 10 minutes / Cook time: 12 minutes

Ingredients:
- 600g salmon fillets
- 60ml teriyaki sauce
- 30ml honey
- 15ml soy sauce
- 2 cloves garlic, minced
- 1 tsp grated ginger
- Sesame seeds and chopped green onions (optional, for garnish)

Preparation instructions:
1. Preheat the Air Fryer to 180°C for 5 minutes.
2. In a bowl, mix teriyaki sauce, honey, soy sauce, minced garlic, and grated ginger to create the marinade.
3. Place salmon fillets in the marinade, ensuring they are coated well. Let them marinate for 10 minutes.
4. Place the marinated salmon fillets in the air fryer basket.
5. Air fry at 180°C for 10-12 minutes, brushing with extra marinade halfway through, until the salmon is cooked to your desired level of doneness.
6. Once cooked, remove the teriyaki glazed salmon fillets from the air fryer. Garnish with sesame seeds and chopped green onions if desired before serving.

Air-Fried Italian Sausage with Peppers and Onions

Serves: 4
Prep time: 10 minutes / Cook time: 20 minutes

Ingredients:
- 500g Italian sausage links
- 2 bell peppers, sliced
- 1 onion, sliced
- 30ml olive oil
- 1 tsp dried oregano
- 1 tsp dried basil
- 1/2 tsp garlic powder

- Salt and black pepper, to taste

Preparation instructions:
1. Preheat the Air Fryer to 180°C for 5 minutes.
2. In a bowl, toss Italian sausage links, sliced bell peppers, sliced onion, olive oil, dried oregano, dried basil, garlic powder, salt, and black pepper until well combined.
3. Place the sausage and vegetable mixture in the air fryer basket.
4. Air fry at 180°C for 18-20 minutes, shaking the basket halfway through the cooking time, until the sausages are cooked through and the vegetables are tender.
5. Once cooked, remove the air-fried Italian sausage with peppers and onions from the air fryer and serve.

Paprika and Cumin Spiced Air-Fried Lamb Chops

Serves: 4
Prep time: 10 minutes / Cook time: 15 minutes

Ingredients:
- 600g lamb chops
- 30ml olive oil
- 1 tsp paprika
- 1 tsp ground cumin
- 1/2 tsp garlic powder
- 1/2 tsp onion powder
- Salt and black pepper, to taste
- Fresh parsley for garnish (optional)

Preparation instructions:
1. Preheat the Air Fryer to 200°C for 5 minutes.
2. In a bowl, coat lamb chops with olive oil, paprika, ground cumin, garlic powder, onion powder, salt, and black pepper.
3. Place the seasoned lamb chops in the air fryer basket.
4. Air fry at 200°C for 12-15 minutes, flipping halfway through the cooking time, until the lamb chops are cooked to your desired level of doneness.
5. Once cooked, remove the paprika and cumin spiced air-fried lamb chops from the air fryer. Garnish with fresh parsley if desired before serving.

Chili-Lime Air-Fried Chicken Thighs

Serves: 4
Prep time: 10 minutes / Cook time: 25 minutes

Ingredients:
- 800g chicken thighs, bone-in and skin-on
- 30ml olive oil
- Zest and juice of 1 lime
- 1 tsp chilli powder
- 1/2 tsp garlic powder
- 1/2 tsp onion powder
- Salt and black pepper, to taste

Preparation instructions:
1. Preheat the Air Fryer to 180°C for 5 minutes.
2. In a bowl, mix olive oil, lime zest, lime juice, chilli powder, garlic powder, onion powder, salt, and black pepper.
3. Rub the chicken thighs with the prepared mixture until evenly coated.
4. Place the seasoned chicken thighs in the air fryer basket.
5. Air fry at 180°C for 20-25 minutes, turning halfway through, until the chicken reaches an internal temperature of 75°C and the skin is crispy.
6. Once cooked, remove the chilli-lime air-fried chicken thighs from the air fryer and let them rest for a few minutes before serving.

Rosemary and Garlic Air-Fried Steak

Serves: 4
Prep time: 10 minutes / Cook time: 12 minutes

Ingredients:
- 600g beef steak (sirloin or ribeye), about 2.5cm thick
- 30ml olive oil
- 2 cloves garlic, minced
- 2 tsp fresh rosemary, chopped
- 1/2 tsp paprika
- Salt and black pepper, to taste

Preparation instructions:
1. Preheat the Air Fryer to 200°C for 5 minutes.
2. Rub the steak with olive oil, minced garlic, chopped rosemary, paprika, salt, and black pepper.
3. Place the seasoned steak in the air fryer basket.
4. Air fry at 200°C for 10-12 minutes, flipping halfway through for even cooking, until the desired level of doneness is reached.
5. Once cooked, remove the rosemary and garlic air-fried steak from the air fryer. Let it rest for a few minutes before slicing and serving.

Honey Mustard Glazed Air-Fried Pork Chops

Serves: 4
Prep time: 10 minutes / Cook time: 18 minutes

Ingredients:
- 600g pork chops
- 60ml honey
- 30ml Dijon mustard
- 15ml olive oil
- 1/2 tsp garlic powder
- Salt and black pepper, to taste

Preparation instructions:
1. Preheat the Air Fryer to 180°C for 5 minutes.
2. In a bowl, mix honey, Dijon mustard, olive oil, garlic powder, salt, and black pepper.
3. Coat the pork chops evenly with the honey mustard mixture.
4. Place the glazed pork chops in the air fryer basket.
5. Air fry at 180°C for 16-18 minutes, flipping halfway through, until the pork chops are cooked through and caramelised.
6. Once cooked, remove the honey mustard glazed air-fried pork chops from the air fryer and let them rest for a few minutes before serving.

Mediterranean Style Air-Fried Lamb Kebabs

Serves: 4
Prep time: 15 minutes / Cook time: 15 minutes

Ingredients:
- 600g lamb leg or shoulder, cubed
- 30ml olive oil
- 2 cloves garlic, minced
- 1 tsp dried oregano
- 1 tsp ground cumin
- 1/2 tsp paprika
- Salt and black pepper, to taste
- Cherry tomatoes, red onion wedges, and bell peppers for skewering

Preparation instructions:
1. Preheat the Air Fryer to 200°C for 5 minutes.
2. In a bowl, combine olive oil, minced garlic, dried oregano, ground cumin, paprika, salt, and black pepper.
3. Thread the cubed lamb, cherry tomatoes, red onion wedges, and bell peppers onto skewers, alternating the ingredients.
4. Brush the Mediterranean-style spice mixture onto the lamb kebabs.
5. Place the kebabs in the air fryer basket.
6. Air fry at 200°C for 12-15 minutes, turning halfway through, until the lamb is cooked to your preferred doneness.
7. Once cooked, remove the Mediterranean-style air-fried lamb kebabs from the air fryer and serve.

Asian-Style Sesame Ginger Air-Fried Beef Stir-Fry

Serves: 4
Prep time: 15 minutes / Cook time: 10 minutes

Ingredients:
- 500g beef strips
- 30ml soy sauce
- 15ml sesame oil
- 15ml rice vinegar
- 2 cloves garlic, minced
- 1 tsp fresh ginger, grated
- 1 tsp honey
- 1/2 tsp red chilli flakes (optional)
- 1 red pepper, sliced
- 1 green pepper, sliced
- 150g broccoli florets
- Sesame seeds, for garnish
- Spring onions, sliced for garnish

Preparation instructions:
1. Preheat the Air Fryer to 200°C for 5 minutes.
2. In a bowl, mix soy sauce, sesame oil, rice vinegar, minced garlic, grated ginger, honey, and red chilli flakes.
3. Marinate the beef strips in this mixture for 10 minutes.
4. Place marinated beef, sliced peppers, and broccoli florets in the air fryer basket.
5. Air fry at 200°C for 8-10 minutes, stirring halfway through, until the beef is cooked and the vegetables are tender.
6. Once cooked, remove the Asian-style sesame ginger air-fried beef stir-fry from the air fryer. Garnish with sesame seeds and spring onions before serving.

BBQ Pulled Chicken Sliders

Serves: 4
Prep time: 10 minutes / Cook time: 20 minutes

Ingredients:
- 500g boneless, skinless chicken breasts
- 120ml BBQ sauce
- 30ml apple cider vinegar
- 15ml Worcestershire sauce
- 1 tbsp brown sugar
- 1/2 tsp garlic powder
- 1/2 tsp onion powder
- Salt and black pepper, to taste
- 4 burger buns
- Coleslaw (optional, for serving)

Preparation instructions:
1. Preheat the Air Fryer to 180°C for 5 minutes.
2. In a bowl, combine BBQ sauce, apple cider vinegar, Worcestershire sauce, brown sugar, garlic powder, onion powder, salt, and black pepper.
3. Place the chicken breasts in the sauce mixture, coating them thoroughly.
4. Transfer the chicken breasts to the air fryer basket.
5. Air fry at 180°C for 18-20 minutes, flipping halfway through, until the chicken is cooked through.
6. Shred the cooked chicken using forks and mix it with any remaining sauce.
7. Assemble the pulled chicken onto burger buns, add coleslaw if desired, and serve as sliders.

Spicy Air-Fried Turkey Breast

Serves: 4
Prep time: 15 minutes / Cook time: 25 minutes

Ingredients:
- 600g turkey breast, boneless and skinless
- 30ml olive oil
- 15ml hot sauce
- 1 tsp paprika
- 1/2 tsp cayenne pepper
- 1/2 tsp garlic powder
- Salt and black pepper, to taste
- Lemon wedges, for serving (optional)

Preparation instructions:
1. Preheat the Air Fryer to 200°C for 5 minutes.
2. In a bowl, combine olive oil, hot sauce, paprika, cayenne pepper, garlic powder, salt, and black pepper.
3. Rub the turkey breast with this spicy mixture, ensuring it's evenly coated.
4. Place the seasoned turkey breast in the air fryer basket.
5. Air fry at 200°C for 20-25 minutes, flipping halfway through, until the turkey is cooked through and golden.
6. Once cooked, remove the spicy air-fried turkey breast from the air fryer. Let it rest for a few minutes before slicing. Serve with lemon wedges if desired.

Lemon Pepper Air-Fried Cod Fillets

Serves: 4
Prep time: 10 minutes / Cook time: 12 minutes

Ingredients:
- 600g cod fillets
- 30ml olive oil
- 2 tsp lemon zest
- 1 tsp black pepper
- 1/2 tsp garlic powder
- 1/2 tsp onion powder
- Salt, to taste
- Fresh parsley, chopped (for garnish, optional)
- Lemon wedges, for serving

Preparation instructions:
1. Preheat the Air Fryer to 200°C for 5 minutes.
2. Pat dry the cod fillets using a paper towel and place them in a shallow dish.
3. In a small bowl, mix olive oil, lemon zest, black pepper, garlic powder, onion powder, and salt.
4. Brush the seasoned mixture onto both sides of the cod fillets.
5. Place the fillets in the air fryer basket.
6. Air fry at 200°C for 10-12 minutes until the cod is cooked through and flakes easily with a fork.
7. Once cooked, garnish with chopped parsley (if desired) and serve with lemon wedges.

Buffalo-Style Air-Fried Turkey Wings

Serves: 4
Prep time: 15 minutes / Cook time: 25 minutes

Ingredients:
- 800g turkey wings
- 60g buffalo sauce
- 30g unsalted butter, melted

- 1 tbsp Worcestershire sauce
- 1/2 tsp garlic powder
- 1/2 tsp onion powder
- Salt and black pepper, to taste
- Ranch or blue cheese dressing (for dipping, optional)

Preparation instructions:
1. Preheat the Air Fryer to 190°C for 5 minutes.
2. Pat dry the turkey wings with paper towels.
3. In a bowl, mix buffalo sauce, melted butter, Worcestershire sauce, garlic powder, onion powder, salt, and black pepper.
4. Toss the turkey wings in this mixture until evenly coated.
5. Place the wings in the air fryer basket in a single layer.
6. Air fry at 190°C for 20-25 minutes, flipping halfway through, until the wings are golden and crispy.
7. Once cooked, serve the buffalo-style air-fried turkey wings with ranch or blue cheese dressing for dipping if desired.

Tandoori Chicken Skewers

Serves: 4
Prep time: 20 minutes / Cook time: 15 minutes

Ingredients:
- 600g boneless chicken thighs, cut into chunks
- 150g plain Greek yoghurt
- 2 tbsp tandoori spice mix
- 1 tbsp lemon juice
- 1 tbsp olive oil
- 2 cloves garlic, minced
- 1 tsp ginger, grated
- Salt, to taste
- Metal or soaked wooden skewers
- Fresh coriander (cilantro), chopped (for garnish, optional)
- Lemon wedges, for serving

Preparation instructions:
1. In a bowl, combine Greek yoghurt, tandoori spice mix, lemon juice, olive oil, minced garlic, grated ginger, and salt.
2. Add the chicken chunks to the marinade, ensuring they're well coated. Marinate in the refrigerator for at least 1 hour or preferably overnight.
3. Preheat the Air Fryer to 200°C for 5 minutes.
4. Thread marinated chicken chunks onto skewers.
5. Place the chicken skewers in the air fryer basket.
6. Air fry at 200°C for 12-15 minutes, turning halfway through, until the chicken is fully cooked.
7. Once cooked, garnish with chopped fresh coriander (if desired) and serve with lemon wedges.

Garlic and Herb Marinated Air-Fried Pork Tenderloin

Serves: 4
Prep time: 15 minutes / Cook time: 20 minutes

Ingredients:
- 600g pork tenderloin
- 3 cloves garlic, minced
- 2 tbsp olive oil
- 1 tbsp fresh thyme, chopped
- 1 tbsp fresh rosemary, chopped
- 1 tsp paprika
- Salt and black pepper, to taste
- Lemon wedges (for serving, optional)

Preparation instructions:
1. In a bowl, combine minced garlic, olive oil, chopped thyme, chopped rosemary, paprika, salt, and black pepper.
2. Rub the pork tenderloin with the prepared herb-garlic mixture, covering it evenly. Marinate in the refrigerator for at least 30 minutes, ideally up to 2 hours.
3. Preheat the Air Fryer to 200°C for 5 minutes.
4. Place the marinated pork tenderloin in the air fryer basket.
5. Air fry at 200°C for 18-20 minutes, turning halfway through, until the pork reaches an internal temperature of 63°C (145°F).
6. Once cooked, let the pork rest for a few minutes before slicing. Serve with lemon wedges if desired.

Italian Seasoned Air-Fried Meatballs

Serves: 4
Prep time: 15 minutes / Cook time: 15 minutes

Ingredients:
- 500g lean ground beef
- 60g breadcrumbs
- 60g grated Parmesan cheese
- 1 egg
- 2 cloves garlic, minced

- 1 tsp dried basil
- 1 tsp dried oregano
- 1/2 tsp onion powder
- Salt and black pepper, to taste
- Marinara sauce (for serving, optional)

Preparation instructions:
1. In a mixing bowl, combine ground beef, breadcrumbs, Parmesan cheese, egg, minced garlic, dried basil, dried oregano, onion powder, salt, and black pepper. Mix until well combined.
2. Shape the mixture into meatballs, about 1-inch in diameter.
3. Preheat the Air Fryer to 180°C for 5 minutes.
4. Place the meatballs in the air fryer basket in a single layer.
5. Air fry at 180°C for 12-15 minutes, shaking the basket halfway through, until the meatballs are cooked through and golden brown.
6. Once cooked, serve the meatballs with marinara sauce if desired.

Crispy Air-Fried Coconut Shrimp

Serves: 4
Prep time: 20 minutes / Cook time: 10 minutes

Ingredients:
- 500g large shrimp, peeled and deveined
- 120g shredded coconut
- 60g breadcrumbs
- 2 eggs, beaten
- 1/2 tsp garlic powder
- 1/2 tsp onion powder
- Salt and black pepper, to taste
- Cooking spray

Preparation instructions:
1. In one bowl, combine shredded coconut and breadcrumbs.
2. In another bowl, beat the eggs and add garlic powder, onion powder, salt, and black pepper.
3. Dip each shrimp into the egg mixture, allowing excess to drip off, then coat it with the coconut-breadcrumb mixture, pressing gently to adhere.
4. Preheat the Air Fryer to 200°C for 5 minutes.
5. Place the coated shrimp in the air fryer basket in a single layer. Lightly spray the shrimp with cooking spray.
6. Air fry at 200°C for 8-10 minutes until the shrimp is golden and crispy.
7. Once cooked, serve the crispy coconut shrimp hot with your preferred dipping sauce.

Moroccan Spiced Air-Fried Chicken Drumsticks

Serves: 4
Prep time: 15 minutes / Cook time: 25 minutes

Ingredients:
- 8 chicken drumsticks
- 2 tbsp olive oil
- 2 cloves garlic, minced
- 1 tsp ground cumin
- 1 tsp ground coriander
- 1 tsp paprika
- 1/2 tsp ground cinnamon
- 1/2 tsp ground ginger
- Salt and black pepper, to taste
- Fresh coriander (cilantro) for garnish (optional)

Preparation instructions:
1. In a bowl, mix olive oil, minced garlic, ground cumin, ground coriander, paprika, ground cinnamon, ground ginger, salt, and black pepper.
2. Score the chicken drumsticks with a sharp knife and rub the spice mixture onto the drumsticks, ensuring they're evenly coated. Marinate in the refrigerator for at least 30 minutes, ideally 2-4 hours.
3. Preheat the Air Fryer to 180°C for 5 minutes.
4. Place the marinated chicken drumsticks in the air fryer basket.
5. Air fry at 180°C for 20-25 minutes, turning halfway through, until the chicken reaches an internal temperature of 75°C (165°F).
6. Once cooked, let them rest for a few minutes. Garnish with fresh coriander if desired before serving.

Honey Sriracha Glazed Air-Fried Turkey Meatloaf

Serves: 4
Prep time: 15 minutes / Cook time: 25 minutes

Ingredients:
- 500g ground turkey
- 120g breadcrumbs
- 60g onion, finely chopped
- 2 cloves garlic, minced
- 2 tbsp honey
- 2 tbsp sriracha sauce
- 1 egg

- 60ml milk
- Salt and black pepper, to taste
- Chopped parsley for garnish (optional)

Preparation instructions:
1. In a bowl, combine ground turkey, breadcrumbs, chopped onion, minced garlic, honey, sriracha sauce, egg, milk, salt, and black pepper. Mix until well combined.
2. Form the mixture into a meatloaf shape.
3. Preheat the Air Fryer to 180°C for 5 minutes.
4. Place the meatloaf in the air fryer basket.
5. Air fry at 180°C for 20-25 minutes until the meatloaf is cooked through and reaches an internal temperature of 75°C (165°F).
6. Once done, let it rest for a few minutes. Garnish with chopped parsley if desired.

Jamaican Jerk Air-Fried Chicken Thighs

Serves: 4
Prep time: 10 minutes / Cook time: 20 minutes

Ingredients:
- 8 bone-in chicken thighs, skin removed
- 2 tbsp Jamaican jerk seasoning
- 2 tbsp olive oil
- Juice of 1 lime
- Salt and black pepper, to taste
- Lime wedges for garnish (optional)

Preparation instructions:
1. In a bowl, mix Jamaican jerk seasoning, olive oil, lime juice, salt, and black pepper.
2. Rub the mixture onto the chicken thighs, ensuring they're evenly coated. Marinate in the refrigerator for at least 1 hour.
3. Preheat the Air Fryer to 200°C for 5 minutes.
4. Place the marinated chicken thighs in the air fryer basket.
5. Air fry at 200°C for 18-20 minutes until the chicken reaches an internal temperature of 75°C (165°F).
6. Once cooked, let them rest for a few minutes before serving. Garnish with lime wedges if desired.

Paprika-Rubbed Air-Fried Beef Sirloin Tips

Serves: 4
Prep time: 10 minutes / Cook time: 12 minutes

Ingredients:
- 500g beef sirloin tips, cut into bite-sized pieces
- 2 tbsp olive oil
- 2 tsp paprika
- 1 tsp garlic powder
- 1 tsp onion powder
- Salt and black pepper, to taste
- Chopped parsley for garnish (optional)

Preparation instructions:
1. In a bowl, combine beef sirloin tips, olive oil, paprika, garlic powder, onion powder, salt, and black pepper. Mix until the beef is well coated.
2. Preheat the Air Fryer to 200°C for 5 minutes.
3. Place the seasoned beef sirloin tips in the air fryer basket.
4. Air fry at 200°C for 10-12 minutes, shaking the basket halfway through the cooking time, until the beef is browned and cooked to your desired level.
5. Once done, let it rest for a couple of minutes. Garnish with chopped parsley if desired before serving.

Air-Fried Stuffed Peppers with Quinoa and Black Beans

Serves: 4
Prep time: 15 minutes / Cook time: 20 minutes

Ingredients:
- 4 large peppers, halved and seeds removed
- 240g cooked quinoa
- 240g black beans, drained and rinsed
- 120g corn kernels
- 120g diced tomatoes
- 60g chopped coriander
- 1 tsp cumin
- 1 tsp chilli powder
- Salt and black pepper, to taste
- 50g shredded cheddar cheese

Preparation instructions:
1. In a bowl, mix together cooked quinoa, black beans, corn kernels, diced tomatoes, chopped coriander, cumin, chilli powder, salt, and black pepper.
2. Stuff each pepper half with the quinoa mixture.
3. Preheat the Air Fryer to 180°C for 5 minutes.
4. Place the stuffed peppers in the air fryer basket.
5. Air fry at 180°C for 18-20 minutes until the peppers are tender.
6. Sprinkle shredded cheddar cheese over the peppers during the last 2-3 minutes of cooking.

7. Once cooked, remove from the air fryer and let cool slightly before serving.

Crispy Tofu and Vegetable Stir-Fry in Air Fryer

Serves: 4
Prep time: 15 minutes / Cook time: 15 minutes

Ingredients:
- 400g firm tofu, drained and cut into cubes
- 2 tbsp soy sauce
- 1 tbsp sesame oil
- 1 tbsp cornstarch
- 1 red pepper, sliced
- 1 green pepper, sliced
- 1 small broccoli head, cut into florets
- 1 carrot, sliced
- 2 spring onions, chopped
- 1 tbsp sesame seeds
- Salt and black pepper, to taste

Preparation instructions:
1. In a bowl, toss tofu cubes with soy sauce, sesame oil, cornstarch, salt, and black pepper until evenly coated.
2. Preheat the Air Fryer to 180°C for 5 minutes.
3. Place the tofu cubes in the air fryer basket and cook at 180°C for 10 minutes, shaking the basket halfway through.
4. Add sliced peppers, broccoli florets, carrot slices, and chopped spring onions to the air fryer basket with the tofu. Toss everything together.
5. Air fry for an additional 5 minutes at 180°C until the vegetables are tender-crisp and tofu is crispy.
6. Sprinkle sesame seeds over the stir-fry before serving.

Courgette Parmesan in the Air Fryer

Serves: 4
Prep time: 15 minutes / Cook time: 10 minutes

Ingredients:
- 2 medium courgettes, sliced into rounds
- 50g grated Parmesan cheese
- 30g breadcrumbs
- 1 tsp dried oregano
- 1/2 tsp garlic powder
- Salt and black pepper, to taste
- Cooking spray or olive oil in a sprayer

Preparation instructions:
1. In a bowl, mix together Parmesan cheese, breadcrumbs, dried oregano, garlic powder, salt, and black pepper.
2. Dip each courgette slice into the mixture, ensuring it's coated on both sides.
3. Preheat the Air Fryer to 200°C for 5 minutes.
4. Place the coated courgette slices in a single layer in the air fryer basket.
5. Spray the slices with cooking spray or olive oil using a sprayer.
6. Air fry at 200°C for 8-10 minutes until golden and crispy.
7. Once done, remove from the air fryer and serve immediately.

Spinach and Mushroom Stuffed Portobello Mushrooms

Serves: 4
Prep time: 15 minutes / Cook time: 12 minutes

Ingredients:
- 4 large Portobello mushrooms
- 100g spinach, chopped
- 100g mushrooms, finely chopped
- 1 garlic clove, minced
- 50g feta cheese, crumbled
- Salt and black pepper, to taste
- Olive oil for drizzling

Preparation instructions:
1. Remove the stems from the Portobello mushrooms and gently scrape out the gills to make space for the stuffing.
2. In a pan, heat a bit of olive oil over medium heat. Sauté the garlic, chopped mushrooms, and spinach until wilted.
3. Season the mixture with salt and black pepper. Remove from heat and let it cool slightly.
4. Preheat the Air Fryer to 180°C for 5 minutes.
5. Stuff each Portobello mushroom with the spinach and mushroom mixture. Top with crumbled feta cheese.
6. Drizzle olive oil over the stuffed mushrooms.
7. Place the mushrooms in the air fryer basket.
8. Air fry at 180°C for 10-12 minutes until the mushrooms are tender and the cheese is lightly browned.
9. Once cooked, remove from the air fryer and serve warm.

Air-Fried Falafel with Tahini Sauce

Serves: 4
Prep time: 20 minutes / Cook time: 15 minutes

Ingredients:
- 400g canned chickpeas, drained and rinsed
- 1 small onion, chopped
- 2 garlic cloves, minced
- 30g fresh parsley, chopped
- 1 tsp ground cumin
- 1 tsp ground coriander
- 1/2 tsp baking powder
- Salt and black pepper, to taste
- Cooking spray or olive oil in a sprayer
- Tahini Sauce:
- 60ml tahini
- 2 tbsp lemon juice
- 2 tbsp water
- 1 garlic clove, minced
- Salt, to taste

Preparation instructions:
1. In a food processor, combine chickpeas, chopped onion, minced garlic, parsley, ground cumin, ground coriander, baking powder, salt, and black pepper. Pulse until the mixture is combined but not completely smooth.
2. Shape the mixture into small balls (falafel).
3. Preheat the Air Fryer to 180°C for 5 minutes.
4. Place the falafel balls in the air fryer basket. Lightly spray them with cooking spray or olive oil using a sprayer.
5. Air fry at 180°C for 12-15 minutes until the falafel are golden and crispy.
6. For the tahini sauce, whisk together tahini, lemon juice, water, minced garlic, and salt in a bowl until smooth.
7. Once the falafel are cooked, remove from the air fryer and serve with the tahini sauce.

Butternut Squash and Chickpea Curry in the Air Fryer

Serves: 4
Prep time: 15 minutes / Cook time: 20 minutes

Ingredients:
- 400g butternut squash, peeled and diced
- 200g chickpeas, drained and rinsed
- 1 onion, finely chopped
- 2 garlic cloves, minced
- 1 tbsp curry powder
- 200ml coconut milk
- 200ml vegetable stock
- Salt and black pepper, to taste
- Fresh coriander (cilantro) for garnish

Preparation instructions:
1. Preheat the Air Fryer to 180°C for 5 minutes.
2. In a bowl, toss the diced butternut squash and chickpeas with curry powder, salt, and black pepper.
3. Place the seasoned squash and chickpeas in the air fryer basket.
4. Air fry at 180°C for 15-18 minutes, shaking halfway through, until the squash is tender and lightly browned.
5. Meanwhile, in a pan over medium heat, sauté the chopped onion and minced garlic until softened.
6. Add the air-fried squash and chickpeas to the pan.
7. Pour in the coconut milk and vegetable stock. Simmer for 5-7 minutes until the sauce thickens.
8. Adjust seasoning if needed, garnish with fresh coriander, and serve hot.

Caprese-Stuffed Air-Fried Courgette Boats

Serves: 4
Prep time: 15 minutes / Cook time: 12 minutes

Ingredients:
- 2 medium courgettes
- 100g cherry tomatoes, halved
- 100g fresh mozzarella, diced
- 2 tbsp fresh basil leaves, chopped
- 1 tbsp olive oil
- Salt and black pepper, to taste
- Balsamic glaze for drizzling (optional)

Preparation instructions:
1. Preheat the Air Fryer to 180°C for 5 minutes.
2. Cut the courgettes in half lengthwise and scoop out the seeds to create a hollow centre.
3. In a bowl, mix together cherry tomatoes, fresh mozzarella, chopped basil, olive oil, salt, and black pepper.
4. Stuff the courgette halves with the tomato and mozzarella mixture.
5. Place the stuffed courgette halves in the air fryer basket.
6. Air fry at 180°C for 10-12 minutes until the courgettes are tender and the cheese is melted.
7. Once cooked, drizzle with balsamic glaze if

desired and serve warm.

Air-Fried Veggie Burger Patties with Sweet Potato Fries

Serves: 4
Prep time: 20 minutes / Cook time: 25 minutes

Ingredients:
- 400g mixed vegetable burger patties (store-bought or homemade)
- 500g sweet potatoes, cut into fries
- 2 tbsp olive oil
- 1/2 tsp paprika
- 1/2 tsp garlic powder
- Salt and black pepper, to taste

Preparation instructions:
1. Preheat the Air Fryer to 200°C for 5 minutes.
2. In a bowl, toss the sweet potato fries with olive oil, paprika, garlic powder, salt, and black pepper.
3. Place the seasoned sweet potato fries in the air fryer basket.
4. Air fry at 200°C for 18-20 minutes, shaking the basket halfway through, until the fries are crispy and golden.
5. Cook the vegetable burger patties in the air fryer according to the package instructions or homemade recipe.
6. Once cooked, serve the veggie burger patties alongside the crispy sweet potato fries.

Mexican-Style Air-Fried Stuffed Poblano Peppers

Serves: 4
Prep time: 15 minutes / Cook time: 20 minutes

Ingredients:
- 4 large poblano peppers
- 200g cooked black beans
- 200g sweetcorn kernels
- 1 small red onion, diced
- 1 tsp ground cumin
- 1 tsp chilli powder
- 100g shredded cheddar cheese
- Fresh coriander for garnish
- Salt and black pepper, to taste
- Olive oil for drizzling

Preparation instructions:
1. Preheat the Air Fryer to 200°C for 5 minutes.
2. Slice the poblano peppers in half lengthwise and remove the seeds.
3. In a bowl, mix together black beans, sweetcorn, diced red onion, ground cumin, chilli powder, salt, and black pepper.
4. Stuff each poblano pepper half with the bean and corn mixture.
5. Place the stuffed peppers in the air fryer basket.
6. Drizzle the peppers with a little olive oil.
7. Air fry at 180°C for 15-18 minutes until the peppers are tender and slightly charred.
8. Sprinkle shredded cheddar cheese on top of each pepper and air fry for an additional 2-3 minutes until the cheese melts.
9. Garnish with fresh coriander and serve hot.

Air-Fried Cauliflower Steaks with Herbed Quinoa Pilaf

Serves: 4
Prep time: 15 minutes / Cook time: 25 minutes

Ingredients:
- 1 large head cauliflower, sliced into steaks
- 100g quinoa, rinsed
- 200ml vegetable broth
- 1 tbsp olive oil
- 1 garlic clove, minced
- 1 tsp dried thyme
- 1 tsp dried parsley
- Zest of 1 lemon
- Salt and black pepper, to taste
- Fresh parsley for garnish

Preparation instructions:
1. Preheat the Air Fryer to 200°C for 5 minutes.
2. In a saucepan, bring the vegetable broth to a boil. Add quinoa, reduce heat to low, cover, and simmer for 15 minutes until the quinoa is cooked and the liquid is absorbed.
3. Meanwhile, brush both sides of cauliflower slices with olive oil and season with minced garlic, dried thyme, dried parsley, lemon zest, salt, and black pepper.
4. Place the cauliflower steaks in the air fryer basket.
5. Air fry at 200°C for 12-15 minutes, flipping halfway through until golden brown and tender.
6. Fluff the cooked quinoa with a fork and mix in fresh parsley.
7. Serve the air-fried cauliflower steaks over the herbed quinoa pilaf and garnish with additional fresh parsley if desired.

Chapter 5: Fish and Seafood

Lemon Herb Air-Fried Tilapia Fillets

Serves: 4
Prep time: 10 minutes / Cook time: 12 minutes

Ingredients:
- 4 tilapia fillets (about 150g each)
- Zest and juice of 1 lemon
- 2 tbsp olive oil
- 2 cloves garlic, minced
- 1 tsp dried thyme
- 1 tsp dried parsley
- Salt and black pepper, to taste
- Lemon wedges, for serving

Preparation instructions:
1. Preheat the Air Fryer to 200°C for 5 minutes.
2. In a bowl, mix together lemon zest, lemon juice, olive oil, minced garlic, dried thyme, dried parsley, salt, and black pepper.
3. Pat dry the tilapia fillets and brush them with the lemon herb mixture.
4. Place the fillets in the air fryer basket.
5. Air fry at 180°C for 10-12 minutes or until the fish is cooked through and easily flakes with a fork.
6. Serve with lemon wedges.

Cajun Spiced Air-Fried Shrimp Skewers

Serves: 4
Prep time: 15 minutes / Cook time: 8 minutes

Ingredients:
- 400g large shrimp, peeled and deveined
- 2 tbsp olive oil
- 1 tbsp Cajun seasoning
- 1 tsp paprika
- 1/2 tsp garlic powder
- 1/2 tsp onion powder
- Salt and black pepper, to taste
- Wooden skewers, soaked in water for 30 minutes

Preparation instructions:
1. Preheat the Air Fryer to 200°C for 5 minutes.
2. In a bowl, combine shrimp, olive oil, Cajun seasoning, paprika, garlic powder, onion powder, salt, and black pepper. Toss to coat the shrimp evenly.
3. Thread the shrimp onto the soaked skewers.
4. Place the skewers in the air fryer basket.
5. Air fry at 200°C for 6-8 minutes, flipping halfway through until the shrimp are pink and opaque.
6. Serve hot.

Garlic Butter Air-Fried Scallops

Serves: 4
Prep time: 10 minutes / Cook time: 6 minutes

Ingredients:
- 400g scallops, cleaned
- 3 tbsp melted butter
- 2 cloves garlic, minced
- 1 tbsp chopped fresh parsley
- 1/2 tsp paprika
- Salt and black pepper, to taste
- Lemon wedges, for serving

Preparation instructions:
1. Preheat the Air Fryer to 200°C for 5 minutes.
2. In a bowl, mix together melted butter, minced garlic, chopped parsley, paprika, salt, and black pepper.
3. Pat dry the scallops and toss them in the garlic butter mixture.
4. Place the scallops in the air fryer basket.
5. Air fry at 200°C for 4-6 minutes until the scallops are cooked through and golden.
6. Serve with lemon wedges.

Teriyaki Glazed Air-Fried Salmon Steaks

Serves: 4
Prep time: 10 minutes / Cook time: 12 minutes

Ingredients:
- 4 salmon steaks (about 150g each)
- 60ml teriyaki sauce
- 1 tbsp honey
- 1 tbsp olive oil
- 2 cloves garlic, minced
- 1 tsp grated ginger
- Sesame seeds, for garnish
- Sliced green onions, for garnish

Preparation instructions:
1. Preheat the Air Fryer to 200°C for 5 minutes.
2. In a bowl, mix teriyaki sauce, honey, olive oil, minced garlic, and grated ginger.
3. Brush both sides of the salmon steaks with the

teriyaki mixture.
4. Place the salmon steaks in the air fryer basket.
5. Air fry at 200°C for 10-12 minutes or until the salmon is cooked through, flipping halfway through the cooking time.
6. Sprinkle sesame seeds and sliced green onions on top before serving.

Crispy Coconut-Crusted Air-Fried Cod Fillets

Serves: 4
Prep time: 15 minutes / Cook time: 10 minutes

Ingredients:
- 4 cod fillets (about 150g each)
- 50g shredded coconut
- 50g panko breadcrumbs
- 2 eggs, beaten
- 1 tbsp olive oil
- 1/2 tsp paprika
- 1/2 tsp garlic powder
- Salt and black pepper, to taste
- Lemon wedges, for serving

Preparation instructions:
1. Preheat the Air Fryer to 200°C for 5 minutes.
2. In a shallow bowl, mix shredded coconut, panko breadcrumbs, paprika, garlic powder, salt, and black pepper.
3. Dip each cod fillet into the beaten eggs, then coat with the coconut breadcrumb mixture.
4. Lightly brush or spray both sides of the coated fillets with olive oil.
5. Place the cod fillets in the air fryer basket.
6. Air fry at 200°C for 8-10 minutes until the coating is crispy and the fish is cooked through.
7. Serve with lemon wedges.

Herbed Lemon Air-Fried Swordfish Steaks

Serves: 4
Prep time: 10 minutes / Cook time: 12 minutes

Ingredients:
- 4 swordfish steaks (about 150g each)
- Zest and juice of 1 lemon
- 2 tbsp olive oil
- 2 cloves garlic, minced
- 1 tsp dried thyme
- 1 tsp dried parsley
- Salt and black pepper, to taste
- Lemon wedges, for serving

Preparation instructions:
1. Preheat the Air Fryer to 200°C for 5 minutes.
2. In a bowl, mix together lemon zest, lemon juice, olive oil, minced garlic, dried thyme, dried parsley, salt, and black pepper.
3. Brush both sides of the swordfish steaks with the herbed lemon mixture.
4. Place the steaks in the air fryer basket.
5. Air fry at 200°C for 10-12 minutes or until the swordfish is cooked through, flipping halfway through the cooking time.
6. Serve with lemon wedges.

Panko-Crusted Air-Fried Haddock Fillets

Serves: 4
Prep time: 15 minutes / Cook time: 10 minutes

Ingredients:
- 4 haddock fillets (about 150g each)
- 50g panko breadcrumbs
- 30g grated Parmesan cheese
- 1 tsp paprika
- 1/2 tsp garlic powder
- 1/2 tsp dried thyme
- Salt and black pepper, to taste
- 2 tbsp olive oil
- Lemon wedges, for serving

Preparation instructions:
1. Preheat the Air Fryer to 200°C for 5 minutes.
2. In a shallow bowl, combine panko breadcrumbs, grated Parmesan cheese, paprika, garlic powder, dried thyme, salt, and black pepper.
3. Brush both sides of the haddock fillets with olive oil.
4. Dip each fillet into the breadcrumb mixture, pressing gently to coat.
5. Place the fillets in the air fryer basket.
6. Air fry at 200°C for 8-10 minutes or until the fish is cooked through and the coating is crispy.
7. Serve with lemon wedges.

Mediterranean Style Air-Fried Sea Bass

Serves: 4
Prep time: 20 minutes / Cook time: 12 minutes

Ingredients:
- 4 sea bass fillets (about 150g each)
- 60g cherry tomatoes, halved
- 40g pitted Kalamata olives, sliced

- 30g crumbled feta cheese
- 2 tbsp olive oil
- 1 tbsp chopped fresh parsley
- 1 tbsp lemon juice
- 2 cloves garlic, minced
- Salt and black pepper, to taste

Preparation instructions:
1. Preheat the Air Fryer to 200°C for 5 minutes.
2. In a bowl, mix cherry tomatoes, Kalamata olives, crumbled feta cheese, olive oil, chopped parsley, lemon juice, minced garlic, salt, and black pepper.
3. Pat dry the sea bass fillets and season with salt and black pepper.
4. Place the seasoned fillets in the air fryer basket.
5. Top each fillet with the Mediterranean mixture.
6. Air fry at 200°C for 10-12 minutes or until the fish is cooked through.
7. Serve the sea bass fillets with the Mediterranean topping.

Lemon Pepper Air-Fried Catfish Nuggets

Serves: 4
Prep time: 15 minutes / Cook time: 10 minutes

Ingredients:
- 450g catfish fillets, cut into nuggets
- 50g cornmeal
- 30g breadcrumbs
- 1 tbsp lemon zest
- 1 tsp ground black pepper
- 1/2 tsp garlic powder
- 1/2 tsp onion powder
- 2 eggs, beaten
- Cooking spray
- Lemon wedges, for serving

Preparation instructions:
1. Preheat the Air Fryer to 200°C for 5 minutes.
2. In a shallow dish, combine cornmeal, breadcrumbs, lemon zest, ground black pepper, garlic powder, and onion powder.
3. Dip the catfish nuggets into the beaten eggs, then coat them with the breadcrumb mixture.
4. Lightly coat the air fryer basket with cooking spray.
5. Place the coated catfish nuggets in the basket.
6. Air fry at 200°C for 8-10 minutes, flipping halfway through, until the nuggets are golden brown and cooked through.
7. Serve with lemon wedges.

Blackened Air-Fried Red Snapper

Serves: 4
Prep time: 15 minutes / Cook time: 10 minutes

Ingredients:
- 4 red snapper fillets (150g each)
- 20g butter, melted
- 2 tsp paprika
- 1 tsp dried thyme
- 1 tsp onion powder
- 1 tsp garlic powder
- 1/2 tsp cayenne pepper
- 1/2 tsp black pepper
- 1/2 tsp salt
- Lemon wedges, for serving

Preparation instructions:
1. Preheat the Air Fryer to 200°C for 5 minutes.
2. In a small bowl, mix melted butter with paprika, dried thyme, onion powder, garlic powder, cayenne pepper, black pepper, and salt.
3. Brush both sides of the red snapper fillets with the butter and spice mixture.
4. Place the fillets in the air fryer basket.
5. Air fry at 200°C for 8-10 minutes or until the fish is cooked through and easily flakes with a fork.
6. Serve with lemon wedges.

Chili-Lime Air-Fried Shrimp Tacos

Serves: 4
Prep time: 20 minutes / Cook time: 8 minutes

Ingredients:
- 400g large shrimp, peeled and deveined
- 8 small corn tortillas
- 1 tbsp olive oil
- 1 tsp chilli powder
- 1/2 tsp garlic powder
- 1/2 tsp onion powder
- 1/2 tsp paprika
- Zest and juice of 1 lime
- Salt and black pepper, to taste
- Toppings: Shredded cabbage, diced tomatoes, chopped cilantro, lime wedges

Preparation instructions:
1. Preheat the Air Fryer to 200°C for 5 minutes.
2. In a bowl, toss the shrimp with olive oil, chilli

powder, garlic powder, onion powder, paprika, lime zest, lime juice, salt, and black pepper.
3. Place the seasoned shrimp in the air fryer basket.
4. Air fry at 200°C for 5-8 minutes or until the shrimp is pink and cooked through.
5. Warm the corn tortillas in the air fryer for 1-2 minutes.
6. Assemble the tacos with the cooked shrimp and desired toppings.

Honey Mustard Glazed Air-Fried Trout Fillets

Serves: 4
Prep time: 15 minutes / Cook time: 10 minutes

Ingredients:
- 4 trout fillets (about 150g each)
- 60ml honey
- 2 tbsp Dijon mustard
- 1 tbsp soy sauce
- 1 tbsp olive oil
- 1 tsp minced garlic
- 1 tsp minced ginger
- Salt and black pepper, to taste
- Chopped fresh parsley, for garnish

Preparation instructions:
1. Preheat the Air Fryer to 190°C for 5 minutes.
2. In a bowl, whisk together honey, Dijon mustard, soy sauce, olive oil, minced garlic, minced ginger, salt, and black pepper.
3. Brush both sides of the trout fillets with the honey mustard mixture.
4. Place the fillets in the air fryer basket.
5. Air fry at 190°C for 8-10 minutes or until the fish is cooked through.
6. Garnish with chopped fresh parsley before serving.

Cajun Seasoned Air-Fried Crawfish

Serves: 4
Prep time: 15 minutes / Cook time: 8 minutes

Ingredients:
- 500g crawfish tails, peeled and deveined
- 30ml olive oil
- 2 tsp paprika
- 1 tsp dried thyme
- 1 tsp garlic powder
- 1 tsp onion powder
- 1/2 tsp cayenne pepper
- 1/2 tsp black pepper
- 1/2 tsp salt
- 1/2 tsp dried oregano
- Lemon wedges, for serving

Preparation instructions:
1. Preheat the Air Fryer to 200°C for 5 minutes.
2. In a bowl, toss the crawfish tails with olive oil, paprika, dried thyme, garlic powder, onion powder, cayenne pepper, black pepper, salt, and dried oregano.
3. Place the seasoned crawfish in the air fryer basket.
4. Air fry at 200°C for 5-8 minutes or until the crawfish tails are cooked through and crispy.
5. Serve with lemon wedges.

Parmesan Crusted Air-Fried Oysters

Serves: 4
Prep time: 20 minutes / Cook time: 10 minutes

Ingredients:
- 500g fresh oysters, shucked
- 100g grated Parmesan cheese
- 50g breadcrumbs
- 2 tbsp melted butter
- 1 tsp garlic powder
- 1 tsp dried parsley
- 1/2 tsp paprika
- Lemon wedges, for serving

Preparation instructions:
1. Preheat the Air Fryer to 200°C for 5 minutes.
2. In a bowl, combine grated Parmesan cheese, breadcrumbs, melted butter, garlic powder, dried parsley, and paprika.
3. Coat each oyster with the Parmesan mixture.
4. Place the coated oysters in the air fryer basket.
5. Air fry at 200°C for 8-10 minutes or until the oysters are crispy and cooked through.
6. Serve with lemon wedges.

Sriracha-Glazed Air-Fried Mahi-Mahi

Serves: 4
Prep time: 15 minutes / Cook time: 12 minutes

Ingredients:
- 4 mahi-mahi fillets (about 150g each)
- 60ml sriracha sauce
- 30ml soy sauce

- 15ml honey
- 1 tbsp olive oil
- 1 tsp minced garlic
- 1 tsp minced ginger
- 1/2 tsp sesame seeds (for garnish)
- Chopped fresh coriander (for garnish)

Preparation instructions:
1. Preheat the Air Fryer to 190°C for 5 minutes.
2. In a bowl, mix sriracha sauce, soy sauce, honey, olive oil, minced garlic, and minced ginger.
3. Brush both sides of the mahi-mahi fillets with the sriracha mixture.
4. Place the fillets in the air fryer basket.
5. Air fry at 190°C for 10-12 minutes or until the fish is cooked through and flakes easily.
6. Garnish with sesame seeds and chopped fresh coriander before serving.

Herb-Marinated Air-Fried Scampi

Serves: 4
Prep time: 15 minutes / Cook time: 10 minutes

Ingredients:
- 500g raw scampi tails, peeled and deveined
- 30ml olive oil
- 2 cloves garlic, minced
- 2 tbsp chopped fresh parsley
- 1 tbsp chopped fresh basil
- 1 tbsp chopped fresh thyme
- 1 tsp lemon zest
- Salt and black pepper, to taste
- Lemon wedges, for serving

Preparation instructions:
1. In a bowl, combine olive oil, minced garlic, chopped parsley, basil, thyme, lemon zest, salt, and black pepper.
2. Add the scampi tails to the herb mixture and toss until well coated.
3. Preheat the Air Fryer to 200°C for 5 minutes.
4. Place the marinated scampi in the Air Fryer basket.
5. Air fry at 200°C for 8-10 minutes or until the scampi is golden and cooked through.
6. Serve hot with lemon wedges.

Crispy Sesame Ginger Air-Fried Tuna Steaks

Serves: 4
Prep time: 20 minutes / Cook time: 10 minutes

Ingredients:
- 4 tuna steaks (about 150g each)
- 45 ml soy sauce
- 15ml sesame oil
- 1 tbsp grated ginger
- 2 cloves garlic, minced
- 1 tbsp honey
- 1 tbsp sesame seeds
- Spring onions, thinly sliced (for garnish)

Preparation instructions:
1. In a bowl, mix soy sauce, sesame oil, grated ginger, minced garlic, and honey.
2. Coat the tuna steaks with the marinade and let them sit for 10 minutes.
3. Preheat the Air Fryer to 200°C for 5 minutes.
4. Place the marinated tuna steaks in the Air Fryer basket.
5. Air fry at 200°C for 8-10 minutes, depending on your preferred doneness.
6. Sprinkle sesame seeds and sliced spring onions on top before serving.

Coconut Lime Air-Fried Shrimp and Pineapple Skewers

Serves: 4
Prep time: 20 minutes / Cook time: 8 minutes

Ingredients:
- 500g large shrimp, peeled and deveined
- 200g pineapple chunks
- 60ml coconut milk
- Zest and juice of 1 lime
- 2 cloves garlic, minced
- 1 tsp paprika
- 1 tsp ground cumin
- Salt and black pepper, to taste
- Wooden skewers, soaked in water

Preparation instructions:
1. In a bowl, mix coconut milk, lime zest, lime juice, minced garlic, paprika, ground cumin, salt, and black pepper.
2. Add shrimp and pineapple chunks to the marinade, tossing to coat evenly. Let it marinate for 10 minutes.
3. Preheat the Air Fryer to 200°C for 5 minutes.
4. Thread marinated shrimp and pineapple alternately onto the skewers.
5. Place the skewers in the Air Fryer basket.
6. Air fry at 200°C for 6-8 minutes or until the

shrimp are pink and cooked through.
7. Serve hot.

Garlic Parmesan Air-Fried Crab Cakes

Serves: 4
Prep time: 15 minutes / Cook time: 10 minutes

Ingredients:
- 450g crab meat
- 60g breadcrumbs
- 30g grated Parmesan cheese
- 1 egg
- 1 tbsp mayonnaise
- 2 cloves garlic, minced
- 1 tsp Dijon mustard
- 2 tbsp chopped parsley
- Salt and black pepper, to taste
- Cooking spray

Preparation instructions:
1. In a bowl, mix crab meat, breadcrumbs, Parmesan cheese, egg, mayonnaise, minced garlic, Dijon mustard, chopped parsley, salt, and black pepper.
2. Form the mixture into patties.
3. Preheat the Air Fryer to 190°C for 5 minutes.
4. Lightly coat the crab cakes with cooking spray.
5. Place the crab cakes in the Air Fryer basket.
6. Air fry at 190°C for 8-10 minutes or until golden brown and cooked through.

Spicy Chipotle Air-Fried Lobster Tails

Serves: 4
Prep time: 15 minutes / Cook time: 8 minutes

Ingredients:
- 4 lobster tails, split in half
- 60ml olive oil
- 2 tbsp chipotle sauce
- 2 cloves garlic, minced
- 1 tsp paprika
- Salt and black pepper, to taste
- Lemon wedges, for serving

Preparation instructions:
1. In a bowl, mix olive oil, chipotle sauce, minced garlic, paprika, salt, and black pepper.
2. Brush the chipotle mixture over the lobster tails.
3. Preheat the Air Fryer to 200°C for 5 minutes.
4. Place the lobster tails in the Air Fryer basket.
5. Air fry at 200°C for 6-8 minutes or until the lobster is opaque and cooked through.
6. Serve with lemon wedges.

Lemon-Herb Air-Fried Mussels

Serves: 4
Prep time: 15 minutes / Cook time: 10 minutes

Ingredients:
- 1kg fresh mussels, cleaned and debearded
- 60ml white wine
- 30ml olive oil
- Zest and juice of 1 lemon
- 2 cloves garlic, minced
- 2 tbsp chopped fresh parsley
- Salt and black pepper, to taste

Preparation instructions:
1. In a bowl, combine white wine, olive oil, lemon zest, lemon juice, minced garlic, chopped parsley, salt, and black pepper.
2. Toss the cleaned mussels in the mixture to coat.
3. Preheat the Air Fryer to 200°C for 5 minutes.
4. Place the mussels in the Air Fryer basket.
5. Air fry at 200°C for 8-10 minutes or until the mussels open and are cooked.

Dill and Garlic Air-Fried Squid Rings

Serves: 4
Prep time: 20 minutes / Cook time: 8 minutes

Ingredients:
- 400g squid rings
- 60g breadcrumbs
- 30g grated Parmesan cheese
- 1 tbsp chopped fresh dill
- 2 cloves garlic, minced
- 1 egg, beaten
- Cooking spray
- Salt and black pepper, to taste

Preparation instructions:
1. In a bowl, mix breadcrumbs, grated Parmesan cheese, chopped dill, minced garlic, salt, and black pepper.
2. Dip the squid rings into beaten egg and then coat them with the breadcrumb mixture.
3. Preheat the Air Fryer to 200°C for 5 minutes.
4. Lightly coat the squid rings with cooking spray.
5. Place the rings in the Air Fryer basket.
6. Air fry at 200°C for 6-8 minutes or until golden and crispy.

Chapter 6: Poultry & Meat Recipes

Honey Garlic Air-Fried Chicken Thighs

Serves: 4
Prep time: 15 minutes / Cook time: 20 minutes

Ingredients:
- 8 bone-in, skin-on chicken thighs
- 60ml honey
- 30ml soy sauce
- 2 cloves garlic, minced
- 15ml olive oil
- 1/2 tsp paprika
- Salt and black pepper, to taste
- Chopped fresh parsley for garnish (optional)

Preparation instructions:
1. In a bowl, mix honey, soy sauce, minced garlic, olive oil, paprika, salt, and black pepper.
2. Pat dry the chicken thighs and brush them with the honey garlic mixture.
3. Preheat the Air Fryer to 180°C for 5 minutes.
4. Place the chicken thighs in the Air Fryer basket.
5. Air fry at 180°C for 18-20 minutes, flipping halfway through, until the chicken reaches an internal temperature of 75°C.
6. Garnish with chopped fresh parsley before serving.

Lemon Herb Air-Fried Turkey Breast

Serves: 4
Prep time: 10 minutes / Cook time: 25 minutes

Ingredients:
- 600g turkey breast, boneless and skinless
- Zest and juice of 1 lemon
- 30ml olive oil
- 2 cloves garlic, minced
- 1 tsp chopped fresh thyme
- 1 tsp chopped fresh rosemary
- Salt and black pepper, to taste

Preparation instructions:
1. In a bowl, combine lemon zest, lemon juice, olive oil, minced garlic, chopped thyme, chopped rosemary, salt, and black pepper.
2. Coat the turkey breast with the lemon herb mixture.
3. Preheat the Air Fryer to 180°C for 5 minutes.
4. Place the turkey breast in the Air Fryer basket.
5. Air fry at 180°C for 25-28 minutes or until the turkey reaches an internal temperature of 75°C.
6. Let it rest for a few minutes before slicing.

Teriyaki Glazed Air-Fried Duck Breast

Serves: 4
Prep time: 15 minutes / Cook time: 18 minutes

Ingredients:
- 600g duck breast fillets
- 60ml teriyaki sauce
- 30ml soy sauce
- 2 tbsp honey
- 1 tbsp rice vinegar
- 1 tsp sesame oil
- 2 cloves garlic, minced
- 1 tsp grated ginger
- Sesame seeds for garnish (optional)
- Chopped spring onions for garnish (optional)

Preparation instructions:
1. In a bowl, mix teriyaki sauce, soy sauce, honey, rice vinegar, sesame oil, minced garlic, and grated ginger.
2. Score the skin of the duck breast and brush it with the teriyaki glaze.
3. Preheat the Air Fryer to 200°C for 5 minutes.
4. Place the duck breast in the Air Fryer basket, skin side up.
5. Air fry at 200°C for 16-18 minutes or until the duck reaches an internal temperature of 60-65°C.
6. Let it rest for a few minutes, slice, and garnish with sesame seeds and chopped spring onions if desired.

BBQ Rubbed Air-Fried Pork Ribs

Serves: 4
Prep time: 15 minutes / Cook time: 40 minutes

Ingredients:
- 800g pork ribs
- 60g BBQ seasoning rub
- Salt and black pepper, to taste
- 30ml olive oil
- BBQ sauce for brushing (optional)

Preparation instructions:
1. Preheat the Air Fryer to 180°C for 5 minutes.
2. Rub the pork ribs with olive oil and season them with BBQ seasoning rub, salt, and black pepper.

3. Place the ribs in the Air Fryer basket.
4. Air fry at 180°C for 35-40 minutes, flipping halfway through. Optionally, brush with BBQ sauce in the last 10 minutes of cooking.

Cajun Spiced Air-Fried Quail

Serves: 4
Prep time: 15 minutes / Cook time: 20 minutes

Ingredients:
- 4 whole quails
- 30g Cajun seasoning
- 30ml olive oil
- Salt and black pepper, to taste
- Lemon wedges for garnish (optional)

Preparation instructions:
1. Preheat the Air Fryer to 200°C for 5 minutes.
2. Rub quails with olive oil, Cajun seasoning, salt, and black pepper.
3. Place the quails in the Air Fryer basket.
4. Air fry at 200°C for 18-20 minutes or until the internal temperature reaches 74°C.

Paprika and Rosemary Air-Fried Lamb Chops

Serves: 4
Prep time: 10 minutes / Cook time: 15 minutes

Ingredients:
- 8 lamb chops
- 30ml olive oil
- 20g paprika
- 2 tbsp fresh rosemary, chopped
- Salt and black pepper, to taste

Preparation instructions:
1. Preheat the Air Fryer to 200°C for 5 minutes.
2. Rub lamb chops with olive oil, paprika, chopped rosemary, salt, and black pepper.
3. Place the lamb chops in the Air Fryer basket.
4. Air fry at 200°C for 12-15 minutes, flipping halfway through, until desired doneness.

Buffalo-Style Air-Fried Chicken Tenders

Serves: 4
Prep time: 15 minutes / Cook time: 15 minutes

Ingredients:
- 500g chicken breast fillets, cut into strips
- 60g buffalo sauce
- 50g breadcrumbs
- 30g grated Parmesan cheese
- Salt and black pepper, to taste
- Cooking spray

Preparation instructions:
1. Preheat the Air Fryer to 200°C for 5 minutes.
2. In a bowl, mix buffalo sauce with chicken strips and let marinate for 10 minutes.
3. In another bowl, combine breadcrumbs, grated Parmesan, salt, and pepper.
4. Coat the marinated chicken strips in the breadcrumb mixture.
5. Place the coated chicken strips in the Air Fryer basket and spray with cooking spray.
6. Air fry at 200°C for 12-15 minutes or until golden and cooked through.

Garlic Parmesan Air-Fried Turkey Meatballs

Serves: 4
Prep time: 15 minutes / Cook time: 15 minutes

Ingredients:
- 500g ground turkey
- 30g breadcrumbs
- 30g grated Parmesan cheese
- 2 cloves garlic, minced
- 2 tbsp fresh parsley, chopped
- 1 large egg
- Salt and black pepper, to taste
- Olive oil spray

Preparation instructions:
1. Preheat the Air Fryer to 180°C for 5 minutes.
2. In a bowl, mix ground turkey, breadcrumbs, grated Parmesan, minced garlic, chopped parsley, egg, salt, and pepper.
3. Form the mixture into meatballs.
4. Place the meatballs in the Air Fryer basket and lightly spray with olive oil.
5. Air fry at 180°C for 12-15 minutes or until meatballs are cooked through and golden.

Moroccan Spiced Air-Fried Lamb Kebabs

Serves: 4
Prep time: 20 minutes / Cook time: 12 minutes

Ingredients:
- 600g lamb leg steak, cubed
- 30ml olive oil
- 2 tsp ground cumin
- 2 tsp paprika
- 1 tsp ground coriander

- 1 tsp ground cinnamon
- Skewers
- Salt and black pepper, to taste

Preparation instructions:
1. Preheat the Air Fryer to 200°C for 5 minutes.
2. In a bowl, mix cubed lamb with olive oil, ground cumin, paprika, ground coriander, ground cinnamon, salt, and pepper.
3. Thread the seasoned lamb onto skewers.
4. Place the lamb skewers in the Air Fryer basket.
5. Air fry at 200°C for 10-12 minutes or until the lamb is cooked to your desired doneness.

Jamaican Jerk Air-Fried Pork Tenderloin

Serves: 4
Prep time: 15 minutes / Cook time: 25 minutes

Ingredients:
- 600g pork tenderloin
- 30ml olive oil
- 2 tbsp Jamaican jerk seasoning
- Salt, to taste

Preparation instructions:
1. Preheat the Air Fryer to 180°C for 5 minutes.
2. Rub the pork tenderloin with olive oil, Jamaican jerk seasoning, and salt.
3. Place the seasoned pork in the Air Fryer basket.
4. Air fry at 180°C for 20-25 minutes or until the internal temperature reaches 63°C (145°F) for medium doneness.
5. Let it rest for a few minutes before slicing.

Herbed Air-Fried Cornish Hens

Serves: 4
Prep time: 20 minutes / Cook time: 30 minutes

Ingredients:
- 2 Cornish hens (approx. 600g each), halved
- 45 ml olive oil
- 2 tsp mixed herbs (rosemary, thyme, sage)
- 2 cloves garlic, minced
- Salt and black pepper, to taste

Preparation instructions:
1. Preheat the Air Fryer to 180°C for 5 minutes.
2. In a bowl, mix olive oil, mixed herbs, minced garlic, salt, and pepper.
3. Rub the herb mixture over the Cornish hen halves.
4. Place the Cornish hen halves in the Air Fryer basket.
5. Air fry at 180°C for 25-30 minutes or until the internal temperature reaches 75°C (165°F).
6. Let them rest for a few minutes before serving.

Chili-Lime Air-Fried Beef Skewers

Serves: 4
Prep time: 25 minutes / Cook time: 10 minutes

Ingredients:
- 600g beef sirloin or steak, cut into cubes
- 30ml olive oil
- Zest and juice of 1 lime
- 2 tsp chilli powder
- 1 tsp cumin powder
- Salt and black pepper, to taste
- Skewers

Preparation instructions:
1. Preheat the Air Fryer to 200°C for 5 minutes.
2. In a bowl, mix olive oil, lime zest, lime juice, chilli powder, cumin powder, salt, and pepper.
3. Thread the beef cubes onto skewers and brush them with the marinade.
4. Place the beef skewers in the Air Fryer basket.
5. Air fry at 200°C for 8-10 minutes or until the beef is cooked to your desired doneness.

Maple Mustard Glazed Air-Fried Ham Steaks

Serves: 4
Prep time: 10 minutes / Cook time: 15 minutes

Ingredients:
- 600g ham steaks
- 60ml maple syrup
- 30ml Dijon mustard
- Salt and black pepper, to taste

Preparation instructions:
1. Preheat the Air Fryer to 180°C for 5 minutes.
2. In a bowl, mix maple syrup, Dijon mustard, salt, and pepper.
3. Brush both sides of the ham steaks with the maple mustard mixture.
4. Place the ham steaks in the Air Fryer basket.
5. Air fry at 180°C for 12-15 minutes, flipping halfway through, until they achieve a caramelised glaze.

Crispy Orange-Glazed Air-Fried Duck Legs

Serves: 4
Prep time: 15 minutes / Cook time: 30 minutes

Ingredients:
- 4 duck legs
- Zest and juice of 1 orange
- 30ml soy sauce
- 30ml honey
- 1 tbsp olive oil
- 2 cloves garlic, minced
- Salt and black pepper, to taste

Preparation instructions:
1. Preheat the Air Fryer to 180°C for 5 minutes.
2. In a bowl, mix orange zest, orange juice, soy sauce, honey, olive oil, minced garlic, salt, and pepper.
3. Score the duck legs and coat them with the orange glaze mixture.
4. Place the duck legs in the Air Fryer basket.
5. Air fry at 180°C for 25-30 minutes, turning halfway through, until crispy and cooked through.

Mediterranean Style Air-Fried Lamb Burgers

Serves: 4
Prep time: 20 minutes / Cook time: 12 minutes

Ingredients:
- 500g ground lamb
- 1/4 red onion, finely chopped
- 1 clove garlic, minced
- 2 tbsp fresh parsley, chopped
- 1 tsp dried oregano
- 1 tsp ground cumin
- Salt and black pepper, to taste

Preparation instructions:
1. Preheat the Air Fryer to 200°C for 5 minutes.
2. In a bowl, mix ground lamb, chopped onion, minced garlic, parsley, oregano, cumin, salt, and pepper. Form into 4 burger patties.
3. Place the lamb burgers in the Air Fryer basket.
4. Air fry at 200°C for 10-12 minutes, flipping halfway through, until they reach your preferred doneness.

Honey Sriracha Air-Fried Chicken Wings

Serves: 4
Prep time: 15 minutes / Cook time: 25 minutes

Ingredients:
- 800g chicken wings
- 60ml honey
- 30ml Sriracha sauce
- 30ml soy sauce
- 2 tbsp olive oil
- 1 tsp garlic powder
- Salt and black pepper, to taste
- Sesame seeds and chopped green onions (optional, for garnish)

Preparation instructions:
1. Preheat the Air Fryer to 200°C for 5 minutes.
2. In a bowl, mix honey, Sriracha sauce, soy sauce, olive oil, garlic powder, salt, and pepper.
3. Toss the chicken wings in the honey Sriracha mixture until coated.
4. Place the wings in the Air Fryer basket.
5. Air fry at 200°C for 20-25 minutes, flipping halfway through, until golden and cooked through. Garnish with sesame seeds and green onions if desired.

Rosemary Balsamic Air-Fried Beef Roast

Serves: 4
Prep time: 10 minutes / Cook time: 25 minutes

Ingredients:
- 600g beef roast
- 60ml balsamic vinegar
- 2 tbsp olive oil
- 2 cloves garlic, minced
- 1 tbsp chopped fresh rosemary
- Salt and black pepper, to taste

Preparation instructions:
1. Preheat the Air Fryer to 200°C for 5 minutes.
2. In a bowl, mix balsamic vinegar, olive oil, minced garlic, chopped rosemary, salt, and pepper.
3. Rub the beef roast with the balsamic mixture.
4. Place the beef roast in the Air Fryer basket.
5. Air fry at 200°C for 20-25 minutes until the internal temperature reaches your desired doneness.

Italian Herb Air-Fried Veal Cutlets

Serves: 4
Prep time: 15 minutes / Cook time: 12 minutes

Ingredients:
- 600g veal cutlets
- 60g breadcrumbs
- 2 tbsp grated Parmesan cheese
- 1 tsp dried Italian herbs
- 1 egg, beaten
- Salt and black pepper, to taste

Preparation instructions:
1. Preheat the Air Fryer to 200°C for 5 minutes.
2. In a bowl, mix breadcrumbs, Parmesan cheese, Italian herbs, salt, and pepper.
3. Dip each veal cutlet in beaten egg, then coat

with the breadcrumb mixture.
4. Place the coated veal cutlets in the Air Fryer basket.
5. Air fry at 200°C for 10-12 minutes, flipping halfway through, until golden and cooked through.

Pesto Marinated Air-Fried Chicken Drumsticks

Serves: 4
Prep time: 20 minutes / Cook time: 25 minutes

Ingredients:
- 800g chicken drumsticks • 60g pesto sauce
- 2 tbsp olive oil • 1 tbsp lemon juice
- 2 cloves garlic, minced
- Salt and black pepper, to taste

Preparation instructions:
1. Preheat the Air Fryer to 200°C for 5 minutes.
2. In a bowl, mix pesto sauce, olive oil, lemon juice, minced garlic, salt, and pepper.
3. Coat the chicken drumsticks with the pesto marinade.
4. Place the drumsticks in the Air Fryer basket.
5. Air fry at 200°C for 20-25 minutes, turning occasionally, until cooked through.

Sesame Ginger Air-Fried Turkey Burgers

Serves: 4
Prep time: 15 minutes / Cook time: 15 minutes

Ingredients:
- 500g ground turkey • 30ml soy sauce
- 2 tbsp sesame oil • 1 tbsp grated ginger
- 2 cloves garlic, minced
- 2 green onions, finely chopped
- 1 tbsp breadcrumbs
- Salt and black pepper, to taste
- Burger buns and desired toppings

Preparation instructions:
1. Preheat the Air Fryer to 190°C for 5 minutes.
2. In a bowl, combine ground turkey, soy sauce, sesame oil, grated ginger, minced garlic, chopped green onions, breadcrumbs, salt, and pepper.
3. Shape the mixture into 4 burger patties.
4. Place the patties in the Air Fryer basket.
5. Air fry at 190°C for 12-15 minutes, flipping halfway through, until cooked through.
6. Serve the burgers on buns with desired toppings.

Lemon Pepper Air-Fried Rabbit

Serves: 4
Prep time: 20 minutes / Cook time: 20 minutes

Ingredients:
- 800g rabbit pieces • 60ml olive oil
- Zest of 1 lemon • 1 tbsp lemon juice
- 2 tsp ground black pepper
- 1 tsp dried thyme • Salt, to taste
- Lemon wedges (for garnish)

Preparation instructions:
1. Preheat the Air Fryer to 180°C for 5 minutes.
2. In a bowl, combine olive oil, lemon zest, lemon juice, black pepper, dried thyme, and salt.
3. Coat the rabbit pieces with the marinade.
4. Place the rabbit in the Air Fryer basket.
5. Air fry at 180°C for 18-20 minutes, turning once, until golden brown and cooked through.
6. Garnish with lemon wedges before serving.

Soy-Garlic Marinated Air-Fried Pork Belly Slices

Serves: 4
Prep time: 15 minutes / Cook time: 20 minutes

Ingredients:
- 600g pork belly slices • 60ml soy sauce
- 2 tbsp honey • 2 cloves garlic, minced
- 1 tsp sesame oil • 1 tsp grated ginger
- 1 tbsp vegetable oil
- Chopped green onions (for garnish)

Preparation instructions:
1. In a bowl, mix soy sauce, honey, minced garlic, sesame oil, and grated ginger.
2. Add the pork belly slices to the marinade, ensuring they're fully coated. Marinate for at least 1 hour.
3. Preheat the Air Fryer to 200°C for 5 minutes.
4. Remove the pork belly slices from the marinade and pat dry with paper towels.
5. Brush the slices with vegetable oil.
6. Place the pork belly in the Air Fryer basket.
7. Air fry at 200°C for 18-20 minutes, flipping halfway through, until crispy and cooked.
8. Garnish with chopped green onions before serving.

Chapter 7: Beans & Legumes

Air-Fried Spiced Chickpea Stuffed Peppers

Serves: 4
Prep time: 15 minutes / Cook time: 20 minutes

Ingredients:
- 4 large peppers
- 400g cooked chickpeas, mashed
- 100g cooked quinoa
- 1 small onion, finely chopped
- 2 cloves garlic, minced
- 1 tsp ground cumin
- 1 tsp paprika
- Salt and black pepper, to taste
- Olive oil (for brushing)

Preparation instructions:
1. Preheat the Air Fryer to 180°C for 5 minutes.
2. Cut the tops off the peppers and remove the seeds and membranes.
3. In a bowl, mix mashed chickpeas, cooked quinoa, chopped onion, minced garlic, ground cumin, paprika, salt, and black pepper.
4. Stuff each pepper with the chickpea mixture.
5. Lightly brush the peppers with olive oil.
6. Place the stuffed peppers in the Air Fryer basket.
7. Air fry at 180°C for 18-20 minutes until the peppers are tender and the filling is heated through.

Air-Fried Black Bean and Quinoa Burgers

Serves: 4
Prep time: 20 minutes (+ chilling time) / Cook time: 15 minutes

Ingredients:
- 400g cooked black beans, mashed
- 100g cooked quinoa
- 1 small onion, finely chopped
- 2 cloves garlic, minced
- 1 tsp ground cumin
- 1 tsp chilli powder
- Salt and black pepper, to taste
- Breadcrumbs
- Olive oil (for brushing)

Preparation instructions:
1. In a bowl, combine mashed black beans, cooked quinoa, chopped onion, minced garlic, ground cumin, chilli powder, salt, and black pepper.
2. Form the mixture into 4 burger patties. Coat each patty lightly with breadcrumbs.
3. Place the patties in the Air Fryer basket and lightly brush with olive oil.
4. Air fry at 190°C for 12-15 minutes, flipping halfway through, until golden brown and cooked through.

Mediterranean Style Air-Fried Lentil Patties

Serves: 4
Prep time: 20 minutes (+ chilling time) / Cook time: 15 minutes

Ingredients:
- 400g cooked lentils, mashed
- 50g breadcrumbs
- 1 small red onion, finely chopped
- 2 cloves garlic, minced
- 1 tsp ground cumin
- 1 tsp dried oregano
- Salt and black pepper, to taste
- Olive oil (for brushing)

Preparation instructions:
1. In a bowl, combine mashed lentils, breadcrumbs, chopped red onion, minced garlic, ground cumin, dried oregano, salt, and black pepper.
2. Shape the mixture into 8 small patties. Refrigerate for 15-20 minutes.
3. Preheat the Air Fryer to 190°C for 5 minutes.
4. Brush the lentil patties lightly with olive oil.
5. Place the patties in the Air Fryer basket.
6. Air fry at 190°C for 12-15 minutes, flipping once, until golden and crispy.

Air-Fried Adzuki Beans with Herbs and Garlic

Serves: 4
Prep time: 10 minutes / Cook time: 20 minutes

Ingredients:
- 400g canned adzuki beans, drained and rinsed
- 2 tbsp olive oil
- 2 cloves garlic, minced
- 1 tsp dried mixed herbs
- Salt and black pepper, to taste

Preparation instructions:
1. Preheat the Air Fryer to 200°C for 5 minutes.
2. In a bowl, toss adzuki beans with olive oil, minced garlic, dried mixed herbs, salt, and black pepper.
3. Place the seasoned beans in the Air Fryer basket.
4. Air fry at 200°C for 15-18 minutes, shaking the basket occasionally, until the beans are crispy and golden.

Cajun Cornbread-Coated Air-Fried Black Eyed Peas

Serves: 4
Prep time: 15 minutes / Cook time: 20 minutes

Ingredients:
- 400g canned black-eyed peas, drained and rinsed
- 100g cornbread mix
- 1 tsp Cajun seasoning
- 2 tbsp olive oil
- Salt, to taste

Preparation instructions:
1. Preheat the Air Fryer to 200°C for 5 minutes.
2. In a bowl, mix cornbread mix and Cajun seasoning.
3. Coat the black-eyed peas in olive oil, then toss them in the cornbread mixture until evenly coated.
4. Place the coated peas in the Air Fryer basket.
5. Air fry at 200°C for 18-20 minutes, shaking the basket occasionally, until crispy and golden.

Smoky Paprika Air-Fried Kidney Beans

Serves: 4
Prep time: 10 minutes / Cook time: 20 minutes

Ingredients:
- 400g canned kidney beans, drained and rinsed
- 2 tbsp olive oil
- 1 tsp smoked paprika
- 1/2 tsp garlic powder
- Salt and black pepper, to taste

Preparation instructions:
1. Preheat the Air Fryer to 200°C for 5 minutes.
2. In a bowl, mix kidney beans with olive oil, smoked paprika, garlic powder, salt, and black pepper.
3. Place the seasoned beans in the Air Fryer basket.
4. Air fry at 200°C for 15-18 minutes, shaking the basket occasionally, until the beans are crispy and lightly browned.

Turmeric and Cumin Spiced Air-Fried Falafel

Serves: 4
Prep time: 15 minutes / Cook time: 15 minutes

Ingredients:
- 400g canned chickpeas, drained and rinsed
- 1 small onion, finely chopped
- 2 garlic cloves, minced
- 2 tbsp chopped fresh parsley
- 1 tsp ground turmeric
- 1 tsp ground cumin
- 2 tbsp plain flour
- Salt and black pepper, to taste
- Olive oil spray

Preparation instructions:
1. Preheat the Air Fryer to 180°C for 5 minutes.
2. In a food processor, blend chickpeas, onion, garlic, parsley, turmeric, cumin, flour, salt, and black pepper until a coarse mixture forms.
3. Shape the mixture into small balls and place them in the Air Fryer basket.
4. Lightly spray the falafel balls with olive oil.
5. Air fry at 180°C for 12-15 minutes until golden brown, flipping halfway through.

Air-Fried Mung Bean Sprouts Salad

Serves: 4
Prep time: 10 minutes / Cook time: 5 minutes

Ingredients:
- 300g mung bean sprouts
- 2 tbsp olive oil

- 1 tbsp soy sauce
- 1 tsp sesame oil
- 1 garlic clove, minced
- 1 tsp grated ginger
- 1 spring onion, finely chopped
- Sesame seeds, for garnish
- Lime wedges, for serving

Preparation instructions:
1. Preheat the Air Fryer to 200°C for 5 minutes.
2. In a bowl, toss mung bean sprouts with olive oil, soy sauce, sesame oil, minced garlic, and grated ginger.
3. Place the seasoned sprouts in the Air Fryer basket.
4. Air fry at 200°C for 4-5 minutes until the sprouts are crispy.
5. Garnish with chopped spring onions and sesame seeds. Serve with lime wedges.

Crispy Garlic Parmesan Air-Fried White Beans

Serves: 4
Prep time: 10 minutes / Cook time: 15 minutes

Ingredients:
- 400g canned white beans, drained and rinsed
- 2 tbsp grated Parmesan cheese
- 2 tbsp olive oil
- 2 cloves garlic, minced
- 1 tsp dried Italian herbs
- Salt and black pepper, to taste

Preparation instructions:
1. Preheat the Air Fryer to 190°C for 5 minutes.
2. In a bowl, mix white beans with grated Parmesan, olive oil, minced garlic, dried Italian herbs, salt, and black pepper.
3. Spread the seasoned beans in the Air Fryer basket.
4. Air fry at 190°C for 12-15 minutes until the beans are crispy and lightly browned.

Harissa Roasted Air-Fried Lima Beans

Serves: 4
Prep time: 10 minutes / Cook time: 15 minutes

Ingredients:
- 400g lima beans, cooked and drained
- 2 tbsp olive oil
- 1-2 tsp harissa paste
- Salt and black pepper, to taste

Preparation instructions:
1. Preheat the Air Fryer to 200°C for 5 minutes.
2. In a bowl, toss cooked lima beans with olive oil, harissa paste, salt, and black pepper.
3. Place the seasoned beans in the Air Fryer basket.
4. Air fry at 200°C for 12-15 minutes until crispy, shaking the basket halfway through.

Herbed Chickpea Fritters in the Air Fryer

Serves: 4
Prep time: 15 minutes / Cook time: 15 minutes

Ingredients:
- 400g canned chickpeas, drained and rinsed
- 1 small onion, finely chopped
- 2 cloves garlic, minced
- 2 tbsp chopped fresh parsley
- 1 tbsp chopped fresh cilantro
- 2 tbsp plain flour
- 1 tsp ground cumin
- Salt and black pepper, to taste
- Olive oil spray

Preparation instructions:
1. Preheat the Air Fryer to 180°C for 5 minutes.
2. In a food processor, blend chickpeas, onion, garlic, parsley, cilantro, flour, cumin, salt, and black pepper until a coarse mixture forms.
3. Shape the mixture into small fritters and place them in the Air Fryer basket.
4. Lightly spray the fritters with olive oil.
5. Air fry at 180°C for 12-15 minutes until golden brown, flipping halfway through.

Air-Fried Split Pea Falafel with Tahini Sauce

Serves: 4
Prep time: 20 minutes / Cook time: 15 minutes

Ingredients:
- For Falafel:
- 400g split peas, soaked and drained
- 1 small onion, chopped
- 3 garlic cloves, minced

- 2 tbsp chopped fresh parsley
- 1 tsp ground cumin
- 1 tsp ground coriander
- Salt and black pepper, to taste
- For Tahini Sauce:
- 4 tbsp tahini paste
- 2 tbsp lemon juice
- 2-3 tbsp water
- 1 garlic clove, minced
- Salt, to taste

Preparation instructions:
- For Falafel:
1. Preheat the Air Fryer to 200°C for 5 minutes.
2. In a food processor, blend split peas, onion, garlic, parsley, cumin, coriander, salt, and black pepper until a coarse mixture forms.
3. Shape the mixture into small balls and place them in the Air Fryer basket.
4. Air fry at 200°C for 12-15 minutes until crispy and cooked through.
- For Tahini Sauce:
1. In a bowl, whisk together tahini paste, lemon juice, water, minced garlic, and salt until smooth.

Sesame Soy Air-Fried Soybean Sprouts

Serves: 4
Prep time: 5 minutes / Cook time: 10 minutes

Ingredients:
- 400g soybean sprouts
- 1 tbsp sesame oil
- 1 tbsp soy sauce
- 1 tsp sesame seeds
- Salt and pepper, to taste

Preparation instructions:
1. Preheat the Air Fryer to 180°C for 5 minutes.
2. In a bowl, toss soybean sprouts with sesame oil, soy sauce, sesame seeds, salt, and pepper.
3. Place the seasoned sprouts in the Air Fryer basket.
4. Air fry at 180°C for 8-10 minutes, shaking the basket halfway through, until crispy.

Air-Fried Black Bean and Sweet Potato Tacos

Serves: 4
Prep time: 15 minutes / Cook time: 20 minutes

Ingredients:
- 400g sweet potatoes, peeled and diced
- 400g canned black beans, drained and rinsed
- 1 tsp chilli powder
- 1 tsp ground cumin
- 1 tsp paprika
- Salt and pepper, to taste
- 8 small corn tortillas
- Toppings: chopped tomatoes, lettuce, avocado, salsa (optional)

Preparation instructions:
1. Preheat the Air Fryer to 200°C for 5 minutes.
2. In a bowl, toss diced sweet potatoes, black beans, chilli powder, cumin, paprika, salt, and pepper.
3. Spread the mixture on the Air Fryer tray.
4. Air fry at 200°C for 18-20 minutes, stirring occasionally, until sweet potatoes are tender.
5. Warm the tortillas in the Air Fryer for 1-2 minutes.
6. Assemble tacos with the cooked mixture and desired toppings.

Pesto Marinated Air-Fried Cannellini Beans

Serves: 4
Prep time: 10 minutes / Cook time: 15 minutes

Ingredients:
- 400g canned cannellini beans, drained and rinsed
- 2 tbsp pesto sauce
- 1 tbsp olive oil
- 1/2 tsp garlic powder
- Salt and pepper, to taste

Preparation instructions:
1. Preheat the Air Fryer to 180°C for 5 minutes.
2. In a bowl, mix cannellini beans with pesto sauce, olive oil, garlic powder, salt, and pepper.
3. Place the coated beans in the Air Fryer basket.
4. Air fry at 180°C for 12-15 minutes until crispy, shaking the basket occasionally.

Air-Fried Refried Beans with Chipotle

Serves: 4
Prep time: 5 minutes / Cook time: 15 minutes

Ingredients:
- 400g canned pinto beans, drained and rinsed

- 1 chipotle pepper in adobo sauce, finely chopped
- 1 tbsp olive oil
- 1/2 tsp ground cumin
- 1/2 tsp chilli powder
- Salt and pepper, to taste

Preparation instructions:
1. Preheat the Air Fryer to 180°C for 5 minutes.
2. In a bowl, mash pinto beans with chipotle pepper, olive oil, ground cumin, chilli powder, salt, and pepper.
3. Place the mashed beans in the Air Fryer basket.
4. Air fry at 180°C for 12-15 minutes until heated through and slightly crispy.

Spicy Curry Air-Fried Adzuki Bean Snack

Serves: 4
Prep time: 5 minutes / Cook time: 15 minutes

Ingredients:
- 400g adzuki beans, cooked and drained
- 2 tbsp olive oil
- 1 tsp curry powder
- 1/2 tsp cayenne pepper
- Salt to taste

Preparation instructions:
1. Preheat the Air Fryer to 180°C for 5 minutes.
2. In a bowl, toss adzuki beans with olive oil, curry powder, cayenne pepper, and salt.
3. Spread the seasoned beans in the Air Fryer basket.
4. Air fry at 180°C for 12-15 minutes, shaking the basket occasionally, until crispy.

Rosemary and Lemon Air-Fried Chickpea Salad

Serves: 4
Prep time: 10 minutes / Cook time: 15 minutes

Ingredients:
- 400g canned chickpeas, drained and rinsed
- 2 tbsp olive oil
- 2 tsp chopped fresh rosemary
- Zest of 1 lemon
- Salt and pepper to taste
- Mixed salad greens

Preparation instructions:
1. Preheat the Air Fryer to 200°C for 5 minutes.
2. In a bowl, toss chickpeas with olive oil, rosemary, lemon zest, salt, and pepper.
3. Place the seasoned chickpeas in the Air Fryer basket.
4. Air fry at 200°C for 12-15 minutes until crispy.
5. Serve over a bed of mixed salad greens.

Air-Fried Lentil and Spinach Stuffed Mushrooms

Serves: 4
Prep time: 15 minutes / Cook time: 20 minutes

Ingredients:
- 12 large mushrooms, stems removed
- 200g cooked lentils
- 100g fresh spinach, chopped
- 50g breadcrumbs
- 1 garlic clove, minced
- 2 tbsp olive oil
- Salt and pepper to taste

Preparation instructions:
1. Preheat the Air Fryer to 180°C for 5 minutes.
2. In a bowl, mix cooked lentils, chopped spinach, breadcrumbs, minced garlic, olive oil, salt, and pepper.
3. Stuff each mushroom cap with the lentil mixture.
4. Place stuffed mushrooms in the Air Fryer basket.
5. Air fry at 180°C for 18-20 minutes until mushrooms are tender and filling is golden.

Crunchy BBQ Seasoned Air-Fried Navy Beans

Serves: 4
Prep time: 5 minutes / Cook time: 15 minutes

Ingredients:
- 400g canned navy beans, drained and rinsed
- 2 tbsp barbecue seasoning
- 1 tbsp olive oil
- Salt to taste

Preparation instructions:
1. Preheat the Air Fryer to 180°C for 5 minutes.
2. In a bowl, toss navy beans with barbecue seasoning, olive oil, and salt.
3. Spread the seasoned beans in the Air Fryer basket.
4. Air fry at 180°C for 12-15 minutes until crispy.

Chapter 8: Healthy Vegetables and Sides

Crispy Air-Fried Brussels Sprouts with Balsamic Glaze

Serves: 4
Prep time: 10 minutes / Cook time: 15 minutes

Ingredients:
- 400g Brussels sprouts, trimmed and halved
- 2 tbsp olive oil
- Salt and black pepper, to taste
- 60ml balsamic glaze

Preparation instructions:
1. Preheat the Air Fryer to 200°C for 5 minutes.
2. In a bowl, toss Brussels sprouts with olive oil, salt, and black pepper.
3. Place Brussels sprouts in the Air Fryer basket.
4. Air fry at 200°C for 12-15 minutes, shaking the basket halfway through.
5. Drizzle balsamic glaze over the cooked Brussels sprouts before serving.

Garlic Parmesan Air-Fried Green Beans

Serves: 4
Prep time: 10 minutes / Cook time: 12 minutes

Ingredients:
- 400g fresh green beans, trimmed
- 2 tbsp olive oil
- 40g grated Parmesan cheese
- 2 cloves garlic, minced
- Salt and black pepper, to taste

Preparation instructions:
1. Preheat the Air Fryer to 190°C for 5 minutes.
2. In a bowl, mix green beans with olive oil, Parmesan cheese, minced garlic, salt, and black pepper.
3. Place the coated green beans in the Air Fryer basket.
4. Air fry at 190°C for 10-12 minutes, shaking the basket halfway through.

Air-Fried Asparagus Wrapped in Prosciutto

Serves: 4
Prep time: 10 minutes / Cook time: 8 minutes

Ingredients:
- 400g asparagus spears, tough ends trimmed
- 8 slices prosciutto
- Olive oil spray
- Black pepper, to taste

Preparation instructions:
1. Preheat the Air Fryer to 200°C for 5 minutes.
2. Bundle 5-6 asparagus spears together and wrap each bundle with a slice of prosciutto.
3. Lightly spray the wrapped asparagus bundles with olive oil.
4. Place the bundles in the Air Fryer basket.
5. Air fry at 200°C for 6-8 minutes until the prosciutto is crisp and the asparagus is tender.

Turmeric Spiced Air-Fried Cauliflower Steaks

Serves: 4
Prep time: 10 minutes / Cook time: 15 minutes

Ingredients:
- 1 large cauliflower head, cut into steaks
- 2 tbsp olive oil
- 1 tsp turmeric powder
- Salt and black pepper, to taste

Preparation instructions:
1. Preheat the Air Fryer to 200°C for 5 minutes.
2. In a bowl, combine olive oil, turmeric powder, salt, and black pepper.
3. Brush both sides of cauliflower steaks with the turmeric mixture.
4. Place the cauliflower steaks in the Air Fryer basket.
5. Air fry at 200°C for 12-15 minutes, flipping halfway through.

Herbed Air-Fried Carrot Fries

Serves: 4
Prep time: 10 minutes / Cook time: 15 minutes

Ingredients:
- 500g carrots, cut into fries
- 2 tbsp olive oil
- 1 tsp dried thyme
- 1 tsp dried rosemary

- Salt and black pepper, to taste

Preparation instructions:
1. Preheat the Air Fryer to 190°C for 5 minutes.
2. In a bowl, toss carrot fries with olive oil, dried thyme, dried rosemary, salt, and black pepper.
3. Place the seasoned carrot fries in the Air Fryer basket.
4. Air fry at 190°C for 12-15 minutes, shaking the basket halfway through.

Panko-Crusted Air-Fried Courgette Chips

Serves: 4
Prep time: 10 minutes / Cook time: 12 minutes

Ingredients:
- 2 medium courgettes, sliced into chips
- 60g panko breadcrumbs
- 2 tbsp grated Parmesan cheese
- 1 tsp paprika
- Olive oil spray
- Salt and black pepper, to taste

Preparation instructions:
1. Preheat the Air Fryer to 200°C for 5 minutes.
2. In a bowl, mix panko breadcrumbs, grated Parmesan cheese, paprika, salt, and black pepper.
3. Coat courgette slices with the breadcrumb mixture.
4. Place the coated courgette chips in the Air Fryer basket and lightly spray with olive oil.
5. Air fry at 200°C for 10-12 minutes, flipping halfway through.

Air-Fried Stuffed Mushrooms with Spinach and Feta

Serves: 4
Prep time: 15 minutes / Cook time: 12 minutes

Ingredients:
- 12 large mushrooms
- 100g fresh spinach, chopped
- 50g feta cheese, crumbled
- 1 garlic clove, minced
- Salt and black pepper, to taste
- Olive oil spray

Preparation instructions:
1. Preheat the Air Fryer to 180°C for 5 minutes.
2. Remove mushroom stems and chop finely. Set aside.
3. In a bowl, mix chopped mushroom stems, chopped spinach, crumbled feta, minced garlic, salt, and black pepper.
4. Stuff each mushroom cap with the spinach-feta mixture.
5. Lightly spray the stuffed mushrooms with olive oil.
6. Place the mushrooms in the Air Fryer basket and air fry at 180°C for 10-12 minutes until tender.

Chili-Lime Air-Fried Corn on the Cob

Serves: 4
Prep time: 5 minutes / Cook time: 12 minutes

Ingredients:
- 4 corn cobs, husked
- 2 tbsp melted butter
- 1 tsp chilli powder
- Zest and juice of 1 lime
- Salt, to taste

Preparation instructions:
1. Preheat the Air Fryer to 200°C for 5 minutes.
2. In a bowl, combine melted butter, chilli powder, lime zest, lime juice, and salt.
3. Brush the seasoned butter mixture onto each corn cob.
4. Place the corn cobs in the Air Fryer basket.
5. Air fry at 200°C for 10-12 minutes, turning halfway through.

Paprika Roasted Air-Fried Broccoli Florets

Serves: 4
Prep time: 10 minutes / Cook time: 8 minutes

Ingredients:
- 500g broccoli florets
- 2 tbsp olive oil
- 1 tsp paprika
- Salt and black pepper, to taste

Preparation instructions:
1. Preheat the Air Fryer to 200°C for 5 minutes.
2. In a bowl, toss broccoli florets with olive oil, paprika, salt, and black pepper.
3. Place the seasoned broccoli florets in the Air Fryer basket.
4. Air fry at 200°C for 6-8 minutes until crispy and lightly browned.

Lemon Herb Air-Fried Artichoke Hearts

Serves: 4
Prep time: 10 minutes / Cook time: 12 minutes

Ingredients:
- 400g canned artichoke hearts, drained and halved
- 2 tbsp olive oil
- 1 lemon (zest and juice)
- 2 cloves garlic, minced
- 1 tsp dried thyme
- Salt and black pepper, to taste

Preparation instructions:
1. Preheat the Air Fryer to 190°C for 5 minutes.
2. In a bowl, combine olive oil, lemon zest, lemon juice, minced garlic, dried thyme, salt, and black pepper.
3. Add the artichoke hearts to the bowl and toss to coat.
4. Place the artichoke hearts in the Air Fryer basket.
5. Air fry at 190°C for 10-12 minutes until golden and slightly crispy.

Parmesan Crusted Air-Fried Acorn Squash Rings

Serves: 4
Prep time: 20 minutes / Cook time: 15 minutes

Ingredients:
- 1 acorn squash, peeled and sliced into rings
- 120g grated Parmesan cheese
- 60g breadcrumbs
- 1 tsp Italian seasoning
- 1/2 tsp garlic powder
- Olive oil spray
- Salt and black pepper, to taste

Preparation instructions:
1. Preheat the Air Fryer to 200°C for 5 minutes.
2. In a bowl, combine grated Parmesan cheese, breadcrumbs, Italian seasoning, garlic powder, salt, and black pepper.
3. Dip each acorn squash ring into the Parmesan mixture, coating both sides.
4. Lightly spray the coated rings with olive oil.
5. Place the squash rings in the Air Fryer basket.
6. Air fry at 200°C for 12-15 minutes until crispy and golden brown.

Balsamic Glazed Air-Fried Aubergine Slices

Serves: 4
Prep time: 15 minutes / Cook time: 15 minutes

Ingredients:
- 2 large aubergines, sliced into rounds
- 3 tbsp balsamic vinegar
- 2 tbsp olive oil
- 1 tsp dried oregano
- 1 tsp garlic powder
- Salt and black pepper, to taste

Preparation instructions:
1. Preheat the Air Fryer to 180°C for 5 minutes.
2. In a bowl, whisk together balsamic vinegar, olive oil, dried oregano, garlic powder, salt, and black pepper.
3. Brush both sides of the aubergine slices with the balsamic mixture.
4. Place the aubergine slices in the Air Fryer basket.
5. Air fry at 180°C for 12-15 minutes, flipping halfway through until tender and caramelised.

Herb-Marinated Air-Fried Tomato Slices

Serves: 4
Prep time: 10 minutes / Cook time: 12 minutes

Ingredients:
- 4 large tomatoes, sliced
- 2 tbsp olive oil
- 2 cloves garlic, minced
- 1 tsp mixed dried herbs (such as thyme, rosemary, oregano)
- Salt and black pepper, to taste

Preparation instructions:
1. Preheat the Air Fryer to 180°C for 5 minutes.
2. In a bowl, combine olive oil, minced garlic, mixed dried herbs, salt, and black pepper.
3. Dip each tomato slice into the herb mixture, coating both sides.
4. Place the tomato slices in the Air Fryer basket.
5. Air fry at 180°C for 10-12 minutes until tender and slightly crispy.

Crispy Garlic-Parmesan Air-Fried Okra

Serves: 4
Prep time: 15 minutes / Cook time: 15 minutes

Ingredients:
- 400g okra, trimmed and halved
- 2 tbsp grated Parmesan cheese
- 2 tbsp breadcrumbs
- 1 tsp garlic powder
- 1/2 tsp paprika
- Olive oil spray
- Salt and black pepper, to taste

Preparation instructions:
1. Preheat the Air Fryer to 200°C for 5 minutes.
2. In a bowl, combine grated Parmesan cheese, breadcrumbs, garlic powder, paprika, salt, and black pepper.
3. Toss the okra in the Parmesan mixture, coating evenly.
4. Place the coated okra in the Air Fryer basket.
5. Lightly spray with olive oil.
6. Air fry at 200°C for 12-15 minutes until golden and crispy.

Turmeric and Cumin Roasted Air-Fried Radishes

Serves: 4
Prep time: 10 minutes / Cook time: 15 minutes

Ingredients:
- 400g radishes, halved
- 2 tbsp olive oil
- 1 tsp ground turmeric
- 1 tsp ground cumin
- 1/2 tsp smoked paprika
- Salt and black pepper, to taste

Preparation instructions:
1. Preheat the Air Fryer to 190°C for 5 minutes.
2. In a bowl, mix olive oil, ground turmeric, ground cumin, smoked paprika, salt, and black pepper.
3. Toss the radishes in the spice mixture until coated.
4. Place the radishes in the Air Fryer basket.
5. Air fry at 190°C for 12-15 minutes until tender and golden.

Crispy Air-Fried Butternut Squash Cubes

Serves: 4
Prep time: 15 minutes / Cook time: 20 minutes

Ingredients:
- 500g butternut squash, peeled and cubed
- 2 tbsp olive oil
- 1 tsp smoked paprika
- 1/2 tsp garlic powder
- Salt and black pepper, to taste

Preparation instructions:
1. Preheat the Air Fryer to 200°C for 5 minutes.
2. In a bowl, toss the butternut squash cubes with olive oil, smoked paprika, garlic powder, salt, and black pepper until evenly coated.
3. Place the seasoned butternut squash in the Air Fryer basket.
4. Air fry at 200°C for 18-20 minutes, shaking halfway through, until crispy and golden brown.

Buffalo Cauliflower Bites in the Air Fryer

Serves: 4
Prep time: 15 minutes / Cook time: 15 minutes

Ingredients:
- 1 medium cauliflower, cut into florets
- 60g buffalo hot sauce
- 2 tbsp melted butter
- 1/2 tsp garlic powder
- 1/2 tsp onion powder
- Salt and black pepper, to taste

Preparation instructions:
1. Preheat the Air Fryer to 190°C for 5 minutes.
2. In a bowl, mix the buffalo hot sauce, melted butter, garlic powder, onion powder, salt, and black pepper.
3. Coat the cauliflower florets with the buffalo sauce mixture.
4. Place the cauliflower florets in the Air Fryer basket.
5. Air fry at 190°C for 12-15 minutes, shaking halfway through, until crispy and slightly charred.

Rosemary Roasted Air-Fried Pepper Strips

Serves: 4
Prep time: 10 minutes / Cook time: 12 minutes

Ingredients:
- 3 peppers (red, yellow, or green), sliced into strips

- 2 tbsp olive oil
- 2 tsp chopped fresh rosemary
- 1/2 tsp smoked paprika
- Salt and black pepper, to taste

Preparation instructions:
1. Preheat the Air Fryer to 180°C for 5 minutes.
2. In a bowl, toss the pepper strips with olive oil, chopped rosemary, smoked paprika, salt, and black pepper.
3. Place the seasoned pepper strips in the Air Fryer basket.
4. Air fry at 180°C for 10-12 minutes until tender and slightly charred.

Lemon-Pepper Air-Fried Sugar Snap Peas

Serves: 4
Prep time: 5 minutes / Cook time: 8 minutes

Ingredients:
- 300g sugar snap peas
- 2 tbsp olive oil
- Zest of 1 lemon
- 1 tsp ground black pepper
- Salt, to taste

Preparation instructions:
1. Preheat the Air Fryer to 180°C for 5 minutes.
2. In a bowl, toss sugar snap peas with olive oil, lemon zest, black pepper, and salt.
3. Place the seasoned sugar snap peas in the Air Fryer basket.
4. Air fry at 180°C for 6-8 minutes until they start to crisp and turn golden.

Air-Fried Ratatouille Medley

Serves: 4
Prep time: 15 minutes / Cook time: 18 minutes

Ingredients:
- 1 medium aubergine, diced
- 1 medium courgette, sliced
- 1 red pepper, diced
- 1 yellow pepper, diced
- 2 tomatoes, diced
- 2 tbsp olive oil
- 2 cloves garlic, minced
- 1 tsp dried basil
- 1 tsp dried oregano
- Salt and black pepper, to taste

Preparation instructions:
1. Preheat the Air Fryer to 200°C for 5 minutes.
2. In a bowl, combine all diced vegetables, olive oil, minced garlic, dried basil, dried oregano, salt, and black pepper. Toss to coat evenly.
3. Place the vegetable mixture in the Air Fryer basket.
4. Air fry at 200°C for 15-18 minutes, shaking occasionally, until vegetables are tender and slightly browned.

Garlic-Herb Air-Fried Parsnip Fries

Serves: 4
Prep time: 10 minutes / Cook time: 18 minutes

Ingredients:
- 500g parsnips, cut into fries
- 2 tbsp olive oil
- 2 cloves garlic, minced
- 1 tsp dried thyme
- 1 tsp dried rosemary
- Salt and black pepper, to taste

Preparation instructions:
1. Preheat the Air Fryer to 190°C for 5 minutes.
2. In a bowl, toss parsnip fries with olive oil, minced garlic, dried thyme, dried rosemary, salt, and black pepper until well coated.
3. Place the parsnip fries in the Air Fryer basket.
4. Air fry at 190°C for 15-18 minutes until golden and crispy, shaking occasionally.

Sesame Ginger Air-Fried Bok Choy

Serves: 4
Prep time: 5 minutes / Cook time: 8 minutes

Ingredients:
- 400g baby bok choy, halved
- 2 tbsp sesame oil
- 1 tbsp soy sauce
- 1 tsp grated ginger
- 1 tsp sesame seeds
- Salt and black pepper, to taste

Preparation instructions:
1. Preheat the Air Fryer to 180°C for 5 minutes.
2. In a bowl, toss bok choy halves with sesame

oil, soy sauce, grated ginger, sesame seeds, salt, and black pepper.
3. Place the seasoned bok choy in the Air Fryer basket.
4. Air fry at 180°C for 6-8 minutes until the bok choy is tender-crisp and slightly browned.

Herb-Marinated Air-Fried Cabbage Wedges

Serves: 4
Prep time: 10 minutes / Cook time: 15 minutes

Ingredients:
- 1 small head cabbage, cut into wedges
- 2 tbsp olive oil
- 2 cloves garlic, minced
- 1 tsp dried thyme
- 1 tsp dried rosemary
- Salt and black pepper, to taste

Preparation instructions:
1. Preheat the Air Fryer to 190°C for 5 minutes.
2. In a bowl, combine olive oil, minced garlic, dried thyme, dried rosemary, salt, and black pepper. Coat the cabbage wedges with this mixture.
3. Place the cabbage wedges in the Air Fryer basket.
4. Air fry at 190°C for 12-15 minutes until the cabbage is tender and slightly crispy.

Crispy Parmesan-Rosemary Air-Fried Potatoes

Serves: 4
Prep time: 10 minutes / Cook time: 20 minutes

Ingredients:
- 600g potatoes, cut into wedges
- 2 tbsp olive oil
- 50g grated Parmesan cheese
- 1 tbsp chopped fresh rosemary
- Salt and black pepper, to taste

Preparation instructions:
1. Preheat the Air Fryer to 200°C for 5 minutes.
2. In a bowl, toss potato wedges with olive oil, grated Parmesan cheese, chopped fresh rosemary, salt, and black pepper until coated.
3. Place the potato wedges in the Air Fryer basket.
4. Air fry at 200°C for 18-20 minutes until the potatoes are crispy and golden.

Mediterranean Style Air-Fried Green Bean Salad

Serves: 4
Prep time: 10 minutes / Cook time: 10 minutes

Ingredients:
- 400g green beans, trimmed
- 2 tbsp olive oil
- 2 tbsp balsamic vinegar
- 1 garlic clove, minced
- 1 tsp dried oregano
- 50g feta cheese, crumbled
- Salt and black pepper, to taste

Preparation instructions:
1. Preheat the Air Fryer to 180°C for 5 minutes.
2. In a bowl, toss green beans with olive oil, balsamic vinegar, minced garlic, dried oregano, salt, and black pepper.
3. Place the seasoned green beans in the Air Fryer basket.
4. Air fry at 180°C for 8-10 minutes until the green beans are tender and slightly charred.
5. Sprinkle it with crumbled feta cheese before serving.

Honey Sriracha Glazed Air-Fried Carrot Coins

Serves: 4
Prep time: 10 minutes / Cook time: 15 minutes

Ingredients:
- 500g carrots, sliced into coins
- 2 tbsp olive oil
- 2 tbsp honey
- 1 tbsp Sriracha sauce
- 1 tbsp soy sauce
- Salt, to taste
- 1 tsp sesame seeds (optional)

Preparation instructions:
1. Preheat the Air Fryer to 190°C for 5 minutes.
2. In a bowl, combine olive oil, honey, Sriracha sauce, soy sauce, and salt. Add carrot coins and toss to coat.
3. Place the carrot coins in the Air Fryer basket.
4. Air fry at 190°C for 12-15 minutes until the carrots are tender and caramelised.
5. Optionally, sprinkle with sesame seeds before serving.

Chapter 9: Fast and Easy Everyday Favourites

Air-Fried Lemon Pepper Chicken Thighs

Serves: 4
Prep time: 10 minutes / Cook time: 20 minutes

Ingredients:
- 600g chicken thighs, bone-in and skin-on
- 2 tbsp olive oil
- Zest of 1 lemon
- 2 tsp black pepper
- 1 tsp garlic powder
- 1 tsp onion powder
- Salt, to taste

Preparation instructions:
1. Preheat the Air Fryer to 200°C for 5 minutes.
2. In a bowl, mix olive oil, lemon zest, black pepper, garlic powder, onion powder, and salt.
3. Pat dry the chicken thighs and coat them with the prepared mixture.
4. Place the chicken thighs in the Air Fryer basket.
5. Air fry at 200°C for 18-20 minutes, flipping halfway through, until the chicken is cooked through and crispy.

Crispy Air-Fried Veggie Spring Rolls

Serves: 4
Prep time: 15 minutes / Cook time: 10 minutes

Ingredients:
- 200g shredded cabbage
- 100g shredded carrots
- 100g bean sprouts
- 8 spring roll wrappers
- 2 tbsp soy sauce
- 1 tbsp sesame oil
- 1 tbsp cornstarch mixed with 2 tbsp water
- Cooking spray

Preparation instructions:
1. In a bowl, mix shredded cabbage, shredded carrots, and bean sprouts.
2. Place a spring roll wrapper on a clean surface. Spoon a portion of the vegetable mixture onto the centre of the wrapper.
3. Fold the sides of the wrapper inward and roll up tightly. Seal the edge with the cornstarch-water mixture.
4. Preheat the Air Fryer to 180°C for 5 minutes.
5. Spray the spring rolls with cooking spray and place them in the Air Fryer basket.
6. Air fry at 180°C for 8-10 minutes until golden and crispy.

BBQ Rubbed Air-Fried Pork Loin Slices

Serves: 4
Prep time: 10 minutes / Cook time: 20 minutes

Ingredients:
- 600g pork loin slices
- 2 tbsp BBQ rub seasoning
- Cooking spray

Preparation instructions:
1. Rub BBQ seasoning evenly over pork loin slices.
2. Preheat the Air Fryer to 200°C for 5 minutes.
3. Lightly spray the pork loin slices with cooking spray.
4. Place the pork loin slices in the Air Fryer basket.
5. Air fry at 200°C for 18-20 minutes until the pork is cooked through and reaches an internal temperature of 145°F (63°C).

Air-Fried Honey Mustard Turkey Breast

Serves: 4
Prep time: 15 minutes / Cook time: 25 minutes

Ingredients:
- 600g turkey breast slices
- 4 tbsp honey
- 2 tbsp Dijon mustard
- 2 tbsp olive oil
- Salt and black pepper, to taste

Preparation instructions:
1. Preheat the Air Fryer to 180°C for 5 minutes.
2. In a bowl, mix honey, Dijon mustard, olive oil, salt, and black pepper.
3. Brush the turkey breast slices with the honey-mustard mixture.
4. Place the turkey breast slices in the Air Fryer basket.
5. Air fry at 180°C for 20-25 minutes until the turkey is cooked through, flipping halfway through.

Teriyaki Glazed Air-Fried Tofu Steaks

Serves: 4
Prep time: 20 minutes / Cook time: 15 minutes

Ingredients:
- 400g firm tofu, sliced into steaks
- 4 tbsp teriyaki sauce
- 2 tbsp soy sauce
- 2 tbsp sesame oil
- 1 tsp garlic powder
- 1 tsp ginger powder
- Sesame seeds (optional)
- Chopped green onions (optional)

Preparation instructions:
1. Press tofu slices between paper towels to remove excess moisture.
2. In a bowl, mix teriyaki sauce, soy sauce, sesame oil, garlic powder, and ginger powder.
3. Coat tofu steaks with the prepared mixture.
4. Preheat the Air Fryer to 200°C for 5 minutes.
5. Place the tofu steaks in the Air Fryer basket.
6. Air fry at 200°C for 12-15 minutes, flipping halfway through, until tofu is golden and slightly crispy.
7. Optionally, sprinkle sesame seeds and chopped green onions before serving.

Herbed Air-Fried Chicken Drumettes

Serves: 4
Prep time: 15 minutes / Cook time: 20 minutes

Ingredients:
- 800g chicken drumettes
- 2 tbsp olive oil
- 2 tsp dried mixed herbs (such as thyme, rosemary, oregano)
- 1 tsp garlic powder
- 1 tsp onion powder
- Salt and black pepper, to taste

Preparation instructions:
1. In a bowl, mix olive oil, dried herbs, garlic powder, onion powder, salt, and black pepper.
2. Coat chicken drumettes with the herb mixture.
3. Preheat the Air Fryer to 200°C for 5 minutes.
4. Place the chicken drumettes in the Air Fryer basket.
5. Air fry at 200°C for 18-20 minutes, turning halfway through, until the chicken is golden and reaches an internal temperature of 165°F (74°C).

Air-Fried Beef and Pepper Skewers

Serves: 4
Prep time: 20 minutes / Cook time: 15 minutes

Ingredients:
- 500g beef steak, cut into cubes
- 2 bell peppers, cut into chunks
- 2 tbsp olive oil
- 2 cloves garlic, minced
- 1 tsp paprika
- Salt and black pepper, to taste
- Skewers (pre-soaked if wooden)

Preparation instructions:
1. In a bowl, mix the olive oil, minced garlic, paprika, salt, and black pepper.
2. Add beef cubes to the mixture, coating them evenly.
3. Thread the marinated beef cubes and bell pepper chunks onto skewers.
4. Preheat the Air Fryer to 200°C for 5 minutes.
5. Place the skewers in the Air Fryer basket.
6. Air fry at 200°C for 12-15 minutes, turning halfway through, until beef is cooked to your desired level.

Parmesan-Herb Air-Fried Tilapia Fillets

Serves: 4
Prep time: 10 minutes / Cook time: 10 minutes

Ingredients:
- 4 tilapia fillets
- 50g grated Parmesan cheese
- 2 tbsp melted butter
- 1 tsp dried herbs (such as thyme, parsley)
- 1 tsp garlic powder
- Salt and black pepper, to taste

Preparation instructions:
1. In a bowl, combine grated Parmesan, melted butter, dried herbs, garlic powder, salt, and black pepper.
2. Coat the tilapia fillets with the Parmesan mixture.
3. Preheat the Air Fryer to 200°C for 5 minutes.
4. Place the coated tilapia fillets in the Air Fryer basket.
5. Air fry at 200°C for 8-10 minutes until the fillets are golden and easily flake with a fork.

Buffalo Cauliflower Florets in the Air Fryer

Serves: 4

Prep time: 15 minutes / Cook time: 15 minutes

Ingredients:
- 1 head cauliflower, cut into florets
- 60g buffalo sauce
- 2 tbsp olive oil
- 1 tsp garlic powder
- Salt and black pepper, to taste
- Ranch or blue cheese dressing (optional, for serving)

Preparation instructions:
1. In a bowl, mix buffalo sauce, olive oil, garlic powder, salt, and black pepper.
2. Toss cauliflower florets in the buffalo sauce mixture until evenly coated.
3. Preheat the Air Fryer to 200°C for 5 minutes.
4. Place the cauliflower florets in the Air Fryer basket.
5. Air fry at 200°C for 12-15 minutes until crispy, shaking the basket halfway through.
6. Serve with ranch or blue cheese dressing if desired.

Pesto Marinated Air-Fried Shrimp Scampi

Serves: 4

Prep time: 15 minutes / Cook time: 10 minutes

Ingredients:
- 400g large shrimp, peeled and deveined
- 3 tbsp pesto sauce
- 2 tbsp olive oil
- 2 cloves garlic, minced
- Zest of 1 lemon
- Salt and black pepper, to taste
- Fresh parsley for garnish

Preparation instructions:
1. In a bowl, mix the shrimp, pesto sauce, olive oil, minced garlic, lemon zest, salt, and black pepper. Let it marinate for 10-15 minutes.
2. Preheat the Air Fryer to 200°C for 5 minutes.
3. Place the marinated shrimp in the Air Fryer basket.
4. Air fry at 200°C for 8-10 minutes or until the shrimp are pink and opaque, shaking the basket halfway through.
5. Garnish with fresh parsley before serving.

Crispy Tofu Nuggets in the Air Fryer

Serves: 4

Prep time: 20 minutes / Cook time: 15 minutes

Ingredients:
- 400g firm tofu, pressed and cut into cubes
- 60g breadcrumbs
- 2 tbsp nutritional yeast (optional)
- 1 tsp garlic powder
- 1 tsp onion powder
- Salt and black pepper, to taste
- Cooking spray or olive oil spray

Preparation instructions:
1. In a bowl, mix breadcrumbs, nutritional yeast (if using), garlic powder, onion powder, salt, and black pepper.
2. Coat tofu cubes with the breadcrumb mixture.
3. Preheat the Air Fryer to 200°C for 5 minutes.
4. Lightly spray the coated tofu cubes with cooking spray or olive oil.
5. Place the tofu cubes in the Air Fryer basket in a single layer.
6. Air fry at 200°C for 12-15 minutes, turning halfway through, until golden and crispy.

Air-Fried Italian Sausage and Veggie Stir-Fry

Serves: 4

Prep time: 15 minutes / Cook time: 15 minutes

Ingredients:
- 400g Italian sausage, sliced
- 200g peppers, sliced
- 200g courgette, sliced
- 150g cherry tomatoes, halved
- 2 tbsp olive oil
- 2 cloves garlic, minced
- 1 tsp Italian seasoning
- Salt and black pepper, to taste

Preparation instructions:
1. In a bowl, toss sliced sausage, peppers, courgette, cherry tomatoes, olive oil, minced garlic, Italian seasoning, salt, and black pepper.
2. Preheat the Air Fryer to 200°C for 5 minutes.
3. Place the mixed ingredients in the Air Fryer basket.
4. Air fry at 200°C for 12-15 minutes, stirring halfway through, until veggies are tender and sausage is cooked through.

Lemon Herb Air-Fried Salmon Steaks

Serves: 4

Prep time: 15 minutes / Cook time: 10 minutes

Ingredients:
- 4 salmon steaks (150g each)
- Zest and juice of 1 lemon
- 2 tbsp olive oil
- 2 cloves garlic, minced
- 1 tsp dried parsley
- Salt and black pepper, to taste
- Lemon wedges for serving

Preparation instructions:
1. In a bowl, mix lemon zest, lemon juice, olive oil, minced garlic, dried parsley, salt, and black pepper.
2. Coat the salmon steaks with the mixture and let them marinate for 10-15 minutes.
3. Preheat the Air Fryer to 200°C for 5 minutes.
4. Place the salmon steaks in the Air Fryer basket.
5. Air fry at 200°C for 8-10 minutes or until the salmon is cooked through.
6. Serve with lemon wedges.

Mediterranean Style Air-Fried Aubergine Slices

Serves: 4
Prep time: 15 minutes / Cook time: 12 minutes

Ingredients:
- 2 large aubergines, sliced into rounds (about 1cm thick)
- 60ml olive oil
- 2 tsp dried oregano
- 2 cloves garlic, minced
- Salt and black pepper, to taste
- Fresh parsley for garnish

Preparation instructions:
1. In a bowl, toss aubergine slices with olive oil, dried oregano, minced garlic, salt, and black pepper.
2. Preheat the Air Fryer to 200°C for 5 minutes.
3. Place the aubergine slices in the Air Fryer basket in a single layer.
4. Air fry at 200°C for 10-12 minutes, flipping halfway through, until golden and tender.
5. Garnish with fresh parsley before serving.

Air-Fried Turkey and Spinach Meatballs

Serves: 4
Prep time: 20 minutes / Cook time: 15 minutes

Ingredients:
- 500g ground turkey
- 100g fresh spinach, finely chopped
- 1 egg
- 50g breadcrumbs
- 2 cloves garlic, minced
- 1 tsp dried basil
- 1 tsp dried oregano
- Salt and black pepper, to taste

Preparation instructions:
1. In a bowl, mix ground turkey, chopped spinach, egg, breadcrumbs, minced garlic, dried basil, dried oregano, salt, and black pepper.
2. Form the mixture into meatballs (about 1.5 inches in diameter).
3. Preheat the Air Fryer to 180°C for 5 minutes.
4. Place the meatballs in the Air Fryer basket.
5. Air fry at 180°C for 12-15 minutes or until the meatballs are cooked through, shaking the basket halfway through.

Coconut-Crusted Air-Fried Shrimp Cakes

Serves: 4
Prep time: 15 minutes / Cook time: 10 minutes

Ingredients:
- 400g cooked shrimp, peeled and deveined
- 50g unsweetened shredded coconut
- 1 large egg
- 2 tbsp coconut flour
- 2 tbsp chopped fresh parsley
- 1 tbsp lime juice
- 1/4 tsp garlic powder
- Salt and black pepper, to taste
- Cooking spray or oil for greasing

Preparation instructions:
1. In a food processor, pulse the shrimp until roughly chopped.
2. In a bowl, combine the chopped shrimp, shredded coconut, egg, coconut flour, chopped parsley, lime juice, garlic powder, salt, and black pepper.
3. Divide the mixture and shape it into patties.
4. Preheat the Air Fryer to 200°C for 5 minutes and lightly grease the Air Fryer basket with cooking spray or oil.
5. Place the shrimp cakes in the basket.
6. Air fry at 200°C for 8-10 minutes, flipping halfway through, until golden brown and cooked through.

Garlic-Rosemary Air-Fried Potato Wedges

Serves: 4
Prep time: 10 minutes / Cook time: 20 minutes

Ingredients:
- 600g potatoes, washed and cut into wedges
- 2 tbsp olive oil
- 2 cloves garlic, minced
- 1 tsp dried rosemary
- Salt and black pepper, to taste

Preparation instructions:
1. In a bowl, toss the potato wedges with olive oil, minced garlic, dried rosemary, salt, and black pepper until evenly coated.
2. Preheat the Air Fryer to 190°C for 5 minutes.
3. Place the potato wedges in the Air Fryer basket.
4. Air fry at 190°C for 18-20 minutes, shaking the basket occasionally, until the wedges are crispy and golden brown.

Air-Fried Falafel Patty Burgers

Serves: 4
Prep time: 20 minutes / Cook time: 12 minutes

Ingredients:
- 400g canned chickpeas, drained and rinsed
- 1 small onion, chopped
- 2 cloves garlic, minced
- 2 tbsp chopped fresh parsley
- 1 tsp ground cumin
- 1 tsp ground coriander
- 1/2 tsp baking powder
- 2 tbsp chickpea flour (besan)
- Salt and black pepper, to taste
- Cooking spray or oil for greasing

Preparation instructions:
1. In a food processor, pulse the chickpeas, onion, garlic, parsley, cumin, coriander, baking powder, chickpea flour, salt, and black pepper until a coarse mixture forms.
2. Form the mixture into patties.
3. Preheat the Air Fryer to 200°C for 5 minutes and lightly grease the Air Fryer basket with cooking spray or oil.
4. Place the falafel patties in the basket.
5. Air fry at 200°C for 10-12 minutes, flipping halfway through, until crispy and golden brown.

Spicy Soy-Glazed Air-Fried Tofu Cubes

Serves: 4
Prep time: 15 minutes / Cook time: 12 minutes

Ingredients:
- 400g firm tofu, pressed and cut into cubes
- 60ml soy sauce
- 30ml maple syrup
- 1 tbsp sesame oil
- 1 tsp sriracha sauce
- 1 clove garlic, minced
- 1/2 tsp grated ginger
- 1/2 tsp red chilli flakes (adjust to taste)
- Sesame seeds and chopped spring onions for garnish

Preparation instructions:
1. In a bowl, mix together soy sauce, maple syrup, sesame oil, sriracha sauce, minced garlic, grated ginger, and red chilli flakes.
2. Add the tofu cubes to the marinade and let it sit for 10 minutes.
3. Preheat the Air Fryer to 200°C for 5 minutes.
4. Place the marinated tofu cubes in the Air Fryer basket.
5. Air fry at 200°C for 10-12 minutes, shaking the basket halfway through cooking, until tofu is crispy and golden brown.
6. Garnish with sesame seeds and chopped spring onions before serving.

Lemon Garlic Air-Fried Cod Fillets

Serves: 4
Prep time: 10 minutes / Cook time: 10 minutes

Ingredients:
- 600g cod fillets
- Zest of 1 lemon
- Juice of 1 lemon
- 2 cloves garlic, minced
- 2 tbsp olive oil
- 1/2 tsp dried thyme
- Salt and black pepper, to taste
- Chopped fresh parsley for garnish

Preparation instructions:
1. In a bowl, mix together the lemon zest, lemon juice, minced garlic, olive oil, dried thyme, salt, and black pepper.
2. Pat dry the cod fillets and brush them with the lemon-garlic marinade.
3. Preheat the Air Fryer to 200°C for 5 minutes.
4. Place the cod fillets in the Air Fryer basket.
5. Air fry at 200°C for 8-10 minutes or until the fish is cooked through and flakes easily with a fork.
6. Garnish with chopped fresh parsley before serving.

Chapter 10: Appetisers

Crispy Air-Fried Courgette Fries with Yoghurt Dip

Serves: 4
Prep time: 15 minutes / Cook time: 12 minutes

Ingredients:
- 2 medium courgettes, cut into thin strips
- 60g breadcrumbs
- 30g grated Parmesan cheese
- 2 large eggs, beaten
- 1/2 tsp garlic powder
- 1/2 tsp paprika
- Salt and black pepper, to taste
- Cooking spray or oil (for air frying)
- Yoghurt Dip:
- 120ml Greek yoghurt
- 1 tbsp lemon juice
- 1 tbsp chopped fresh parsley
- 1/2 tsp garlic powder
- Salt and black pepper, to taste

Preparation instructions:
1. Preheat the Air Fryer to 200°C for 5 minutes.
2. In a bowl, mix breadcrumbs, grated Parmesan cheese, garlic powder, paprika, salt, and black pepper.
3. Dip courgette strips into beaten eggs, then coat them in the breadcrumb mixture.
4. Place the coated courgette strips in the Air Fryer basket, making sure they're in a single layer and not touching.
5. Air fry at 200°C for 10-12 minutes until golden brown and crispy.
6. For the yoghurt dip, mix together Greek yoghurt, lemon juice, chopped parsley, garlic powder, salt, and black pepper.
7. Serve the crispy courgette fries with the yoghurt dip.

Air-Fried Stuffed Jalapeño Poppers with Cream Cheese

Serves: 4
Prep time: 20 minutes / Cook time: 10 minutes

Ingredients:
- 8 large jalapeño peppers, halved and deseeded
- 100g cream cheese
- 50g shredded cheddar cheese
- 1/4 tsp garlic powder
- 1/4 tsp onion powder
- Salt and black pepper, to taste
- 30g breadcrumbs
- Cooking spray or oil (for air frying)

Preparation instructions:
1. Preheat the Air Fryer to 180°C for 5 minutes.
2. In a bowl, mix cream cheese, shredded cheddar cheese, garlic powder, onion powder, salt, and black pepper.
3. Stuff each jalapeño half with the cream cheese mixture.
4. Roll the stuffed jalapeños in breadcrumbs to coat them evenly.
5. Lightly spray or brush the Air Fryer basket with oil, then place the stuffed jalapeños inside.
6. Air fry at 180°C for 8-10 minutes until the jalapeños are tender and the filling is golden brown.

Parmesan-Crusted Air-Fried Cauliflower Bites

Serves: 4
Prep time: 15 minutes / Cook time: 15 minutes

Ingredients:
- 1 medium cauliflower head, cut into florets
- 50g grated Parmesan cheese
- 30g breadcrumbs
- 1 tsp garlic powder
- 1 tsp dried thyme
- Salt and black pepper, to taste
- 2 large eggs, beaten
- Cooking spray or oil (for air frying)

Preparation instructions:
1. Preheat the Air Fryer to 190°C for 5 minutes.
2. In a bowl, mix grated Parmesan cheese, breadcrumbs, garlic powder, dried thyme, salt, and black pepper.
3. Dip cauliflower florets into beaten eggs, then coat them in the Parmesan breadcrumb mixture.
4. Place the coated cauliflower florets in the Air Fryer basket, ensuring they're in a single layer.
5. Air fry at 190°C for 12-15 minutes until the cauliflower is tender and the coating is crispy.

Garlic-Herb Air-Fried Mushrooms Stuffed with Spinach and Cheese

Serves: 4

Prep time: 15 minutes / Cook time: 12 minutes

Ingredients:
- 16 large mushrooms, stems removed
- 100g fresh spinach, chopped
- 100g grated mozzarella cheese
- 50g grated Parmesan cheese
- 2 cloves garlic, minced
- 2 tbsp olive oil
- Salt and black pepper, to taste
- Cooking spray or oil (for air frying)

Preparation instructions:
1. Preheat the Air Fryer to 180°C for 5 minutes.
2. In a bowl, mix chopped spinach, mozzarella cheese, Parmesan cheese, minced garlic, olive oil, salt, and black pepper.
3. Stuff each mushroom cap with the spinach-cheese mixture.
4. Lightly spray or brush the Air Fryer basket with oil, then place the stuffed mushrooms inside.
5. Air fry at 180°C for 10-12 minutes until the mushrooms are tender and the cheese is melted and slightly golden.

Air-Fried Buffalo Chicken Wings with Greek Yoghurt Ranch Dip

Serves: 4

Prep time: 10 minutes / Cook time: 25 minutes

Ingredients:
- 900g chicken wings
- 60ml hot sauce (like Frank's RedHot)
- 60g unsalted butter, melted
- 1/2 tsp garlic powder
- 1/2 tsp onion powder
- Salt and black pepper, to taste
- Cooking spray or oil (for air frying)
- Greek Yoghurt Ranch Dip:
- 120ml Greek yoghurt
- 1 tbsp lemon juice • 1 tsp dried dill
- 1 tsp dried parsley • 1/2 tsp garlic powder
- Salt and black pepper, to taste

Preparation instructions:
1. Preheat the Air Fryer to 200°C for 5 minutes.
2. Pat dry the chicken wings and season them with salt and black pepper.
3. In a bowl, mix hot sauce, melted butter, garlic powder, onion powder, salt, and black pepper.
4. Toss the chicken wings in the sauce mixture until evenly coated.
5. Lightly spray or brush the Air Fryer basket with oil, then place the wings inside.
6. Air fry at 200°C for 22-25 minutes, flipping halfway through, until crispy and cooked through.
7. For the dip, combine Greek yoghurt, lemon juice, dried dill, dried parsley, garlic powder, salt, and black pepper.

Crispy Coconut Shrimp with Mango Dipping Sauce

Serves: 4

Prep time: 20 minutes / Cook time: 10 minutes

Ingredients:
- 400g large shrimp, peeled and deveined
- 50g all-purpose flour
- 2 large eggs, beaten
- 100g shredded coconut
- Cooking spray or oil (for air frying)
- Mango Dipping Sauce:
- 1 ripe mango, peeled and diced
- 2 tbsp lime juice • 1 tbsp honey
- 1/2 tsp chilli flakes (optional)
- 1 tbsp chopped fresh coriander (cilantro)

Preparation instructions:
1. Preheat the Air Fryer to 200°C for 5 minutes.
2. Dredge the shrimp in flour, dip in beaten eggs, then coat with shredded coconut.
3. Place the coated shrimp in the Air Fryer basket in a single layer.
4. Lightly spray or brush the shrimp with oil.
5. Air fry at 200°C for 8-10 minutes until golden and crispy.
6. For the mango dipping sauce, blend diced mango, lime juice, honey, chilli flakes (if using), and chopped coriander until smooth.

Lemon Pepper Air-Fried Artichoke Hearts

Serves: 4

Prep time: 15 minutes / Cook time: 12 minutes

Ingredients:
- 400g canned or jarred artichoke hearts, drained and halved• 30ml olive oil

- 1 tbsp lemon juice
- 1/2 tsp lemon zest
- 1/2 tsp black pepper
- 1/4 tsp garlic powder
- Salt, to taste
- Cooking spray or oil (for air frying)

Preparation instructions:
1. Preheat the Air Fryer to 180°C for 5 minutes.
2. In a bowl, toss the artichoke hearts with olive oil, lemon juice, lemon zest, black pepper, garlic powder, and salt.
3. Lightly spray or brush the Air Fryer basket with oil, then place the seasoned artichoke hearts inside.
4. Air fry at 180°C for 10-12 minutes until they are tender and lightly browned.

Spicy Sriracha Air-Fried Tofu Bites

Serves: 4
Prep time: 20 minutes / Cook time: 15 minutes

Ingredients:
- 400g firm tofu, pressed and cubed
- 2 tbsp cornflour (cornstarch)
- 2 tbsp Sriracha sauce
- 1 tbsp soy sauce
- 1/2 tsp garlic powder
- 1 tbsp olive oil
- 1/2 tsp onion powder
- 1/4 tsp paprika
- Salt, to taste
- Cooking spray or oil (for air frying)

Preparation instructions:
1. Preheat the Air Fryer to 200°C for 5 minutes.
2. In a bowl, coat the tofu cubes with cornflour, Sriracha sauce, soy sauce, olive oil, garlic powder, onion powder, paprika, and salt.
3. Lightly spray or brush the Air Fryer basket with oil, then place the tofu cubes inside.
4. Air fry at 200°C for 12-15 minutes, shaking halfway through, until the tofu is crispy and golden brown.

Mediterranean Style Air-Fried Falafel with Tahini Sauce

Serves: 4
Prep time: 20 minutes / Cook time: 15 minutes

Ingredients:
- 400g canned chickpeas, drained and rinsed
- 1 small onion, finely chopped
- 2 cloves garlic, minced
- 2 tbsp chopped fresh parsley
- 2 tbsp chopped fresh coriander (cilantro)
- 1 tsp ground cumin
- 1 tsp ground coriander
- 2 tbsp plain flour
- Salt and black pepper, to taste
- Cooking spray or oil (for air frying)
- Tahini Sauce:
- 60ml tahini
- 60ml water
- 2 tbsp lemon juice
- 1 clove garlic, minced
- Salt, to taste

Preparation instructions:
1. Preheat the Air Fryer to 190°C for 5 minutes.
2. In a food processor, combine chickpeas, onion, garlic, parsley, coriander, cumin, ground coriander, flour, salt, and black pepper. Pulse until combined but still slightly chunky.
3. Form the mixture into small balls and lightly flatten to shape into patties.
4. Lightly spray or brush the Air Fryer basket with oil, then place the falafel patties inside.
5. Air fry at 190°C for 12-15 minutes, turning halfway through, until golden brown and crispy.
6. For the tahini sauce, whisk together tahini, water, lemon juice, minced garlic, and salt until smooth.

Crispy Onion Rings in the Air Fryer with Spicy Aioli

Serves: 4
Prep time: 15 minutes / Cook time: 10 minutes

Ingredients:
- 2 large onions, cut into rings
- 100g plain flour
- 2 large eggs, beaten
- 150g breadcrumbs
- 1 tsp paprika
- 1/2 tsp garlic powder
- Salt and black pepper, to taste
- Cooking spray or oil (for air frying)
- Spicy Aioli:
- 4 tbsp mayonnaise
- 1 tbsp Sriracha sauce
- 1 clove garlic, minced
- 1/2 tsp lemon juice
- Salt, to taste

Preparation instructions:
1. Preheat the Air Fryer to 200°C for 5 minutes.

2. In three separate bowls, place the flour in one, beaten eggs in another, and mix breadcrumbs with paprika, garlic powder, salt, and black pepper in the third.
3. Coat each onion ring in flour, dip into the beaten eggs, then coat with the breadcrumb mixture.
4. Lightly spray or brush the Air Fryer basket with oil, then arrange the coated onion rings inside.
5. Air fry at 200°C for 8-10 minutes until golden and crispy.
6. Meanwhile, prepare the spicy aioli by combining mayonnaise, Sriracha sauce, minced garlic, lemon juice, and salt. Serve with the onion rings.

Teriyaki Glazed Air-Fried Meatballs

Serves: 4
Prep time: 20 minutes / Cook time: 15 minutes

Ingredients:
- 500g minced meat (beef or pork)
- 50ml teriyaki sauce
- 30g breadcrumbs
- 1 egg
- 2 cloves garlic, minced
- 2 spring onions, finely chopped
- Salt and black pepper, to taste
- Cooking spray or oil (for air frying)

Preparation instructions:
1. Preheat the Air Fryer to 180°C for 5 minutes.
2. In a bowl, mix together the minced meat, teriyaki sauce, breadcrumbs, egg, minced garlic, chopped spring onions, salt, and black pepper.
3. Form the mixture into small meatballs.
4. Lightly spray or brush the Air Fryer basket with oil, then place the meatballs inside.
5. Air fry at 180°C for 12-15 minutes until the meatballs are cooked through and golden brown.

Herbed Air-Fried Potato Skins with Turkey Bacon

Serves: 4
Prep time: 25 minutes / Cook time: 20 minutes

Ingredients:
- 4 large potatoes
- 60g grated cheddar cheese
- 4 slices turkey bacon, cooked and crumbled
- 2 tbsp chopped fresh chives
- 1 tbsp olive oil
- 1/2 tsp garlic powder
- 1/2 tsp onion powder
- Salt and black pepper, to taste
- Cooking spray or oil (for air frying)

Preparation instructions:
1. Preheat the Air Fryer to 200°C for 5 minutes.
2. Scrub potatoes and dry thoroughly. Pierce each potato several times with a fork and rub with olive oil.
3. Air fry potatoes at 200°C for 35-40 minutes or until tender.
4. Let the potatoes cool slightly. Slice each potato in half lengthwise and scoop out the flesh, leaving about 1/4 inch of potato on the skin.
5. In a bowl, mix the potato flesh with grated cheddar cheese, crumbled turkey bacon, chopped chives, garlic powder, onion powder, salt, and black pepper.
6. Lightly spray or brush the Air Fryer basket with oil, then stuff the potato skins with the mixture.
7. Air fry at 200°C for 10-12 minutes until the cheese is melted and the skins are crispy.

Cajun Spiced Air-Fried Okra Fritters

Serves: 4
Prep time: 15 minutes / Cook time: 10 minutes

Ingredients:
- 250g okra, sliced
- 50g gram flour (chickpea flour)
- 2 tbsp cornmeal
- 1 tsp Cajun seasoning
- 1/2 tsp garlic powder
- Salt and black pepper, to taste
- Cooking spray or oil (for air frying)

Preparation instructions:
1. Preheat the Air Fryer to 200°C for 5 minutes.
2. In a bowl, combine the sliced okra, gram flour, cornmeal, Cajun seasoning, garlic powder, salt, and black pepper.
3. Toss the okra slices until evenly coated with the flour mixture.
4. Lightly spray or brush the Air Fryer basket

with oil, then place the okra slices inside.
5. Air fry at 200°C for 8-10 minutes until crispy and golden brown.

Air-Fried Stuffed Cherry Tomatoes with Herbed Goat Cheese

Serves: 4
Prep time: 20 minutes / Cook time: 5 minutes

Ingredients:
- 16 cherry tomatoes
- 100g goat cheese
- 2 tbsp fresh herbs (parsley, chives), finely chopped
- Salt and black pepper, to taste
- Cooking spray or oil (for air frying)

Preparation instructions:
1. Preheat the Air Fryer to 180°C for 5 minutes.
2. Slice the top of each cherry tomato and scoop out the seeds to create a cavity.
3. In a bowl, mix the goat cheese, fresh herbs, salt, and black pepper.
4. Stuff each cherry tomato with the goat cheese mixture.
5. Lightly spray or brush the Air Fryer basket with oil, then place the stuffed tomatoes inside.
6. Air fry at 180°C for 4-5 minutes until the tomatoes are slightly softened and the cheese is lightly browned.

Pesto Mozzarella-Stuffed Air-Fried Portobello Mushrooms

Serves: 4
Prep time: 25 minutes / Cook time: 15 minutes

Ingredients:
- 4 large portobello mushrooms
- 100g mozzarella cheese, sliced
- 4 tbsp pesto sauce
- 2 tbsp breadcrumbs
- Cooking spray or oil (for air frying)

Preparation instructions:
1. Preheat the Air Fryer to 180°C for 5 minutes.
2. Remove the stems from the portobello mushrooms and scrape out the gills using a spoon.
3. Spread 1 tablespoon of pesto inside each mushroom cap.
4. Place a slice of mozzarella inside each mushroom on top of the pesto.
5. Sprinkle breadcrumbs over the cheese.
6. Lightly spray or brush the Air Fryer basket with oil, then place the mushrooms inside.
7. Air fry at 180°C for 12-15 minutes until the cheese is melted and bubbly.

Garlic Parmesan Air-Fried Green Beans

Serves: 4
Prep time: 10 minutes / Cook time: 8 minutes

Ingredients:
- 400g fresh green beans, trimmed
- 2 tbsp olive oil
- 50g grated Parmesan cheese
- 2 cloves garlic, minced
- 1/2 tsp salt
- 1/4 tsp black pepper

Preparation instructions:
1. Preheat the Air Fryer to 200°C for 5 minutes.
2. In a bowl, toss the green beans with olive oil, minced garlic, salt, and black pepper until evenly coated.
3. Place the seasoned green beans in the Air Fryer basket.
4. Air fry at 200°C for 8 minutes, shaking the basket halfway through cooking.
5. Sprinkle grated Parmesan over the green beans and air fry for an additional minute until the cheese is melted and slightly crispy.

Crispy Thai-Style Air-Fried Spring Rolls with Dipping Sauce

Serves: 4
Prep time: 30 minutes / Cook time: 10 minutes

Ingredients:
- 12 spring roll wrappers
- 200g vermicelli rice noodles, cooked and cooled
- 240g shredded cabbage
- 1 carrot, julienned
- 1 red pepper, thinly sliced
- 1 tbsp soy sauce
- 1 tbsp sesame oil
- Cooking spray or oil (for air frying)
- Sweet chilli sauce or dipping sauce of choice

Preparation instructions:
1. In a large bowl, combine the cooked vermicelli

noodles, shredded cabbage, carrot, red pepper, soy sauce, and sesame oil. Mix well.
2. Place a portion of the vegetable mixture onto each spring roll wrapper. Roll tightly, tucking in the sides, and seal the edges with water.
3. Lightly spray or brush the Air Fryer basket with oil and place the spring rolls inside.
4. Air fry at 180°C for 10 minutes, turning halfway through, until the rolls are golden brown and crispy.
5. Serve the crispy spring rolls with sweet chilli sauce or your preferred dipping sauce.

Air-Fried Greek Spanakopita Triangles

Serves: 4
Prep time: 20 minutes / Cook time: 12 minutes

Ingredients:
- 250g fresh spinach, chopped
- 100g feta cheese, crumbled
- 50g ricotta cheese
- 1/2 onion, finely chopped
- 2 cloves garlic, minced
- 1 tsp olive oil
- 12 sheets filo pastry
- Cooking spray or oil (for air frying)

Preparation instructions:
1. Heat olive oil in a pan over medium heat. Sauté the onion and garlic until softened.
2. Add chopped spinach to the pan and cook until wilted. Remove from heat and let it cool.
3. In a bowl, mix the cooked spinach, feta cheese, and ricotta cheese until well combined.
4. Take one sheet of filo pastry, brush it lightly with oil, and place another sheet on top. Cut the sheets lengthwise into three strips.
5. Place a spoonful of the spinach mixture at one end of each strip. Fold into triangles, continuing to the end of the strip.
6. Lightly spray or brush the Air Fryer basket with oil and place the triangles inside.
7. Air fry at 180°C for 12 minutes until the triangles are golden and crispy.

Lemon Herb Air-Fried Avocado Fries

Serves: 4
Prep time: 15 minutes / Cook time: 10 minutes

Ingredients:
- 2 avocados, ripe but firm
- 50g breadcrumbs
- Zest of 1 lemon
- 1/2 tsp dried thyme
- 1/2 tsp dried parsley
- 1/4 tsp garlic powder
- 1/4 tsp onion powder
- Salt and black pepper, to taste
- Cooking spray or oil (for air frying)

Preparation instructions:
1. Preheat the Air Fryer to 200°C for 5 minutes.
2. Cut the avocados into slices or wedges, discarding the skin and pit.
3. In a bowl, mix breadcrumbs, lemon zest, thyme, parsley, garlic powder, onion powder, salt, and black pepper.
4. Coat each avocado slice with the breadcrumb mixture.
5. Lightly spray or brush the Air Fryer basket with oil and place the avocado slices inside.
6. Air fry at 200°C for 10 minutes, flipping halfway through, until crispy and golden brown.

Balsamic Glazed Air-Fried Brussels Sprouts with Cranberries

Serves: 4
Prep time: 10 minutes / Cook time: 15 minutes

Ingredients:
- 400g Brussels sprouts, trimmed and halved
- 50g dried cranberries
- 2 tbsp balsamic glaze
- 1 tbsp olive oil
- 1/2 tsp garlic powder
- Salt and black pepper, to taste

Preparation instructions:
1. Preheat the Air Fryer to 180°C for 5 minutes.
2. In a bowl, toss the Brussels sprouts with olive oil, garlic powder, salt, and black pepper.
3. Place the Brussels sprouts in the Air Fryer basket.
4. Air fry at 180°C for 10 minutes, shaking the basket halfway through cooking.
5. Add dried cranberries to the Brussels sprouts, toss, and air fry for an additional 5 minutes.
6. Drizzle balsamic glaze over the cooked Brussels sprouts and cranberries before serving.

Chapter 11: Sweet Snacks and Desserts

Cinnamon Sugar Air-Fried Apple Slices

Serves: 4
Prep time: 10 minutes / Cook time: 10 minutes

Ingredients:
- 4 medium apples, cored and sliced
- 1 tbsp lemon juice
- 1 tsp ground cinnamon
- 1 tbsp granulated sugar or sweetener of choice

Preparation instructions:
1. Preheat the Air Fryer to 180°C for 5 minutes.
2. In a bowl, toss apple slices with lemon juice to prevent browning.
3. In a separate bowl, mix cinnamon and sugar.
4. Coat the apple slices with the cinnamon-sugar mixture.
5. Place the apple slices in the Air Fryer basket.
6. Air fry at 180°C for 8-10 minutes until golden and slightly crispy.

Air-Fried Banana Chips with Cacao Drizzle

Serves: 4
Prep time: 5 minutes / Cook time: 10 minutes

Ingredients:
- 4 ripe bananas, thinly sliced
- 2 tbsp cacao powder
- 1 tbsp maple syrup or sweetener of choice

Preparation instructions:
1. Preheat the Air Fryer to 160°C for 5 minutes.
2. Place banana slices in a single layer in the Air Fryer basket.
3. Air fry at 160°C for 8-10 minutes until the banana slices turn crispy.
4. In a bowl, mix cacao powder and maple syrup to create a drizzle.
5. Drizzle the cacao mixture over the air-fried banana chips.

Almond Flour Air-Fried Donuts with Sugar-Free Glaze

Serves: 4
Prep time: 15 minutes / Cook time: 8 minutes

Ingredients for Donuts:
- 150g almond flour
- 2 large eggs
- 2 tbsp unsweetened almond milk
- 2 tbsp melted coconut oil
- 1/4 tsp baking powder
- 1/4 tsp vanilla extract
- 1/4 tsp ground cinnamon
- Pinch of salt
- Sweetener to taste (optional)
- Ingredients for Sugar-Free Glaze:
- 2 tbsp powdered erythritol or sweetener of choice
- 1 tbsp unsweetened almond milk

Preparation instructions for Donuts:
1. Preheat the Air Fryer to 180°C for 5 minutes.
2. In a bowl, mix almond flour, eggs, almond milk, melted coconut oil, baking powder, vanilla extract, cinnamon, salt, and sweetener.
3. Spoon the batter into a greased donut pan that fits inside the Air Fryer.
4. Air fry at 180°C for 6-8 minutes until the donuts are firm and golden.
- Preparation instructions for Sugar-Free Glaze:
1. In a small bowl, whisk powdered erythritol and almond milk until smooth.
2. Drizzle the glaze over the cooled almond flour donuts.

Air-Fried Strawberry Shortcake Skewers

Serves: 4
Prep time: 15 minutes / Cook time: 10 minutes

Ingredients:
- 400g fresh strawberries, hulled
- 4 slices pound cake, cut into cubes
- 60 ml melted butter
- 2 tbsp granulated sugar

- 1/2 tsp ground cinnamon

Preparation instructions:
1. Preheat the Air Fryer to 180°C for 5 minutes.
2. In a bowl, mix melted butter, sugar, and cinnamon.
3. Thread strawberries and pound cake cubes onto skewers, alternating.
4. Brush the skewers with the butter mixture.
5. Air fry at 180°C for 8-10 minutes until lightly browned.

Chocolate-Dipped Air-Fried Coconut Macaroons

Serves: 4
Prep time: 10 minutes / Cook time: 10 minutes

Ingredients:
- 100g shredded coconut
- 60ml sweetened condensed milk
- 30g almond flour
- 60g dark chocolate, melted

Preparation instructions:
1. Preheat the Air Fryer to 160°C for 5 minutes.
2. In a bowl, mix shredded coconut, sweetened condensed milk, and almond flour.
3. Form small macaroon balls and place them in the Air Fryer basket.
4. Air fry at 160°C for 8-10 minutes until golden.
5. Dip cooled macaroons into melted chocolate and let them set.

Vanilla Cinnamon Air-Fried Pear Slices

Serves: 4
Prep time: 10 minutes / Cook time: 8 minutes

Ingredients:
- 4 ripe pears, sliced
- 1 tbsp honey
- 1 tsp vanilla extract
- 1/2 tsp ground cinnamon

Preparation instructions:
1. Preheat the Air Fryer to 180°C for 5 minutes.
2. In a bowl, mix honey, vanilla extract, and ground cinnamon.
3. Toss pear slices in the honey mixture.
4. Place pear slices in the Air Fryer basket.
5. Air fry at 180°C for 6-8 minutes until tender and slightly caramelised.

Air-Fried Pineapple Rings with Honey Lime Drizzle

Serves: 4
Prep time: 10 minutes / Cook time: 8 minutes

Ingredients:
- 4 slices fresh pineapple, cored and cut into rings
- 2 tbsp honey
- Zest and juice of 1 lime

Preparation instructions:
1. Preheat the Air Fryer to 180°C for 5 minutes.
2. In a bowl, mix honey, lime zest, and lime juice.
3. Brush both sides of pineapple rings with the honey-lime mixture.
4. Place pineapple rings in the Air Fryer basket.
5. Air fry at 180°C for 6-8 minutes until golden and slightly caramelised.

Lemon Poppy Seed Air-Fried Muffins

Makes: 4 muffins
Prep time: 10 minutes / Cook time: 15 minutes

Ingredients:
- 100g self-raising flour
- 40g granulated sugar
- Zest of 1 lemon
- 1 tbsp poppy seeds
- 60ml milk
- 30ml vegetable oil
- 1 large egg

Preparation instructions:
1. Preheat the Air Fryer to 180°C for 5 minutes.
2. In a bowl, combine flour, sugar, lemon zest, and poppy seeds.
3. In another bowl, whisk together milk, vegetable oil, and egg.
4. Pour the wet ingredients into the dry ingredients and mix until just combined.
5. Divide the batter into 4 silicone muffin cups.
6. Place the muffin cups in the Air Fryer basket.
7. Air fry at 180°C for 12-15 minutes until a toothpick comes out clean when inserted into the muffins.

Hazelnut Cocoa Air-Fried Granola Clusters

Serves: 4
Prep time: 10 minutes / Cook time: 15 minutes

Ingredients:
- 100g rolled oats
- 40g chopped hazelnuts
- 2 tbsp cocoa powder
- 30ml maple syrup
- 2 tbsp melted coconut oil

Preparation instructions:
1. Preheat the Air Fryer to 160°C for 5 minutes.
2. In a bowl, mix rolled oats, chopped hazelnuts, and cocoa powder.
3. Drizzle maple syrup and melted coconut oil over the mixture and toss until coated.
4. Spread the mixture evenly in the Air Fryer basket.
5. Air fry at 160°C for 12-15 minutes, shaking the basket occasionally, until crisp and golden.
6. Allow the granola clusters to cool before serving.

Pumpkin Spice Air-Fried Sweet Potato Chips

Serves: 4
Prep time: 15 minutes / Cook time: 15 minutes

Ingredients:
- 400g sweet potatoes, thinly sliced
- 2 tbsp olive oil
- 1 tsp pumpkin spice mix
- Salt, to taste

Preparation instructions:
1. Preheat the Air Fryer to 180°C for 5 minutes.
2. In a bowl, toss sweet potato slices with olive oil, pumpkin spice mix, and salt.
3. Place the seasoned sweet potato slices in the Air Fryer basket in a single layer.
4. Air fry at 180°C for 12-15 minutes, flipping halfway through, until crispy.

Air-Fried Blueberry Almond Crisp

Serves: 4
Prep time: 10 minutes / Cook time: 20 minutes

Ingredients:
- 200g fresh blueberries
- 50g rolled oats
- 30g almond flour
- 30g sliced almonds
- 2 tbsp honey
- 2 tbsp melted butter

Preparation instructions:
1. Preheat the Air Fryer to 180°C for 5 minutes.
2. In a bowl, mix blueberries with 1 tbsp honey.
3. In another bowl, combine oats, almond flour, sliced almonds, melted butter, and remaining honey.
4. Place the blueberries in a baking dish, sprinkle the oat-almond mixture over them.
5. Air fry at 180°C for 18-20 minutes until the top is golden brown and the blueberries are bubbling.

Honey Caramelized Air-Fried Nectarines

Serves: 4
Prep time: 10 minutes / Cook time: 10 minutes

Ingredients:
- 4 nectarines, sliced
- 2 tbsp honey

Preparation instructions:
1. Preheat the Air Fryer to 180°C for 5 minutes.
2. Toss nectarine slices with honey in a bowl until coated.
3. Place the nectarine slices in the Air Fryer basket.
4. Air fry at 180°C for 8-10 minutes until caramelised, shaking the basket halfway through.

Chocolate Hazelnut Stuffed Air-Fried Dates

Serves: 4
Prep time: 10 minutes / Cook time: 5 minutes

Ingredients:
- 12 large Medjool dates, pitted
- 4 tsp chocolate hazelnut spread
- 20g chopped hazelnuts (optional)

Preparation instructions:
1. Preheat the Air Fryer to 180°C for 5 minutes.

2. Stuff each date with 1/3 teaspoon of chocolate hazelnut spread and sprinkle chopped hazelnuts on top.
3. Place the stuffed dates in the Air Fryer basket.
4. Air fry at 180°C for 4-5 minutes until the dates are slightly caramelised.

Air-Fried Raspberry Oatmeal Bars

Serves: 4
Prep time: 15 minutes / Cook time: 20 minutes

Ingredients:
- 200g rolled oats
- 80g raspberry jam
- 40g almond flour
- 30g melted coconut oil
- 30g honey
- 50g fresh raspberries

Preparation instructions:
1. Preheat the Air Fryer to 180°C for 5 minutes.
2. In a bowl, combine rolled oats, almond flour, melted coconut oil, and honey.
3. Press half of the oat mixture into the bottom of an Air Fryer-safe baking dish.
4. Spread raspberry jam over the oat layer.
5. Sprinkle fresh raspberries on top.
6. Crumble the remaining oat mixture over the raspberries.
7. Air fry at 180°C for 18-20 minutes until golden brown.

Maple Cinnamon Air-Fried Plantain Chips

Serves: 4
Prep time: 10 minutes / Cook time: 15 minutes

Ingredients:
- 2 large ripe plantains
- 2 tbsp maple syrup
- 1 tsp cinnamon

Preparation instructions:
1. Preheat the Air Fryer to 180°C for 5 minutes.
2. Peel the plantains and thinly slice them.
3. In a bowl, toss plantain slices with maple syrup and cinnamon until evenly coated.
4. Place the coated plantain slices in the Air Fryer basket in a single layer.
5. Air fry at 180°C for 12-15 minutes, flipping halfway through, until crispy.

Chai Spiced Air-Fried Pears with Greek Yoghurt

Serves: 4
Prep time: 10 minutes / Cook time: 10 minutes

Ingredients:
- 4 ripe pears, sliced
- 2 tbsp honey
- 1 tsp chai spice mix (cinnamon, cardamom, cloves, ginger)
- 200g Greek yoghurt

Preparation instructions:
1. Preheat the Air Fryer to 180°C for 5 minutes.
2. In a bowl, toss pear slices with honey and chai spice mix until coated.
3. Place the coated pear slices in the Air Fryer basket.
4. Air fry at 180°C for 8-10 minutes until the pears are tender and slightly caramelised.
5. Serve with Greek yoghurt.

Almond Butter Stuffed Air-Fried Apples

Serves: 4
Prep time: 15 minutes / Cook time: 10 minutes

Ingredients:
- 4 large apples
- 4 tbsp almond butter
- 2 tbsp maple syrup
- 1 tsp ground cinnamon

Preparation instructions:
1. Core the apples, leaving the bottoms intact.
2. Mix almond butter, maple syrup, and cinnamon in a bowl.
3. Stuff each apple with a tablespoon of the almond butter mixture.
4. Place the stuffed apples in the Air Fryer basket.
5. Air fry at 180°C for 10-12 minutes until the apples are tender.

Coconut Flour Air-Fried Brownies with Walnuts

Serves: 4
Prep time: 15 minutes / Cook time: 20 minutes

Ingredients:
- 60g coconut flour
- 40g cocoa powder
- 4 tbsp melted coconut oil
- 80ml maple syrup
- 4 large eggs
- 60ml unsweetened almond milk
- 50g chopped walnuts

Preparation instructions:
1. Preheat the Air Fryer to 180°C for 5 minutes.
2. In a bowl, mix coconut flour, cocoa powder, melted coconut oil, maple syrup, eggs, and almond milk until smooth.
3. Fold in chopped walnuts into the batter.
4. Pour the batter into a greased Air Fryer baking pan.
5. Air fry at 180°C for 18-20 minutes until the brownies are set.
6. Let them cool before slicing.

Orange Glazed Air-Fried Peach Slices

Serves: 4
Prep time: 10 minutes / Cook time: 10 minutes

Ingredients:
- 4 large peaches, sliced
- 60ml orange juice
- Zest of 1 orange
- 2 tbsp honey or maple syrup
- 1 tsp cornstarch

Preparation instructions:
1. Preheat the Air Fryer to 180°C for 5 minutes.
2. In a bowl, mix orange juice, orange zest, honey or maple syrup, and cornstarch.
3. Toss peach slices in the mixture until coated.
4. Place the coated peaches in the Air Fryer basket.
5. Air fry at 180°C for 8-10 minutes until the peaches are tender and glazed.

Peanut Butter Banana Air-Fried Spring Rolls

Serves: 4
Prep time: 15 minutes / Cook time: 10 minutes

Ingredients:
- 8 spring roll wrappers
- 2 ripe bananas, sliced
- 120g peanut butter
- 2 tbsp honey or agave syrup
- Cooking spray or oil for brushing

Preparation instructions:
1. Preheat the Air Fryer to 180°C for 5 minutes.
2. Lay a spring roll wrapper flat and spread a teaspoon of peanut butter onto the wrapper.
3. Place a few banana slices on the peanut butter side and drizzle with honey or agave syrup.
4. Roll up the wrapper, folding in the sides, and brush the edges with water to seal.
5. Repeat with the remaining wrappers.
6. Lightly spray or brush the rolls with cooking oil.
7. Place the rolls in the Air Fryer basket without touching each other.
8. Air fry at 180°C for 8-10 minutes until golden and crispy.

References

21 Diabetes-Friendly Recipes You Can Make in the Air Fryer. (n.d.). EatingWell. https://www.eatingwell.com/gallery/7989033/diabetes-friendly-air-fryer-recipes/

Air Fryer Diabetes Recipes. (n.d.). Taste of Home. https://www.tasteofhome.com/collection/air-fryer-diabetic-recipes/

Diabetes recipes. (n.d.). BBC Food. https://www.bbc.co.uk/food/collections/diabetes_recipes

Diabetes UK. (2022). Types of diabetes. Diabetes UK. https://www.diabetes.org.uk/diabetes-the-basics/types-of-diabetes

NHS. (2023, March 6). Diabetes. NHS; NHS. https://www.nhs.uk/conditions/diabetes/

RD, A. C., MS. (2022, March 3). The Ultimate Guide to Low Carb Air Fryer Recipes for Diabetes. Amanda Ciprich. https://www.t1dnutritionist.com/post/the-ultimate-guide-to-low-carb-air-fryer-recipes-for-diabetes

What to Eat With Diabetes. (n.d.). Info.diatribe.org. https://info.diatribe.org/what-to-eat-with-diabetes/?msclkid=0d98565996f41d55a45b33d6924f50e9&utm_source=bing&utm_medium=cpc&utm_campaign=1.1-%20Articles&utm_term=what%20can%20diabetes%20eat&utm_content=What%20to%20eat%20Diabetes

30-Day Meal Plan

	Breakfast	**Lunch**	**Dinner**	**Snack/Dessert**
Day 1	Air Fryer Veggie Omelette	Air-Fried Lemon Herb Chicken Breasts	Lemon Herb Air-Fried Turkey Breast	Cinnamon Sugar Air-Fried Apple Slices
Day 2	Crispy Turkey Bacon	Lemon Herb Air-Fried Tilapia Fillets	Crispy Tofu and Vegetable Stir-Fry in Air Frye	Air-Fried Banana Chips with Cacao Drizzle
Day 3	Low-Carb Breakfast Burritos	Garlic Parmesan Air-Fried Crab Cakes	Cajun Spiced Air-Fried Shrimp Skewers	Almond Flour Air-Fried Donuts with Sugar-Free Glaze
Day 4	Air-Fried Avocado and Egg	Turkey Meatballs with Marinara Sauce	Honey Garlic Air-Fried Chicken Thighs	Air-Fried Strawberry Shortcake Skewers
Day 5	Cinnamon Apple Chips	Garlic Butter Air-Fried Scallops	Courgette Parmesan in the Air Frye	Chocolate-Dipped Air-Fried Coconut Macaroons
Day 6	Sweet Potato Hash Browns	Teriyaki Glazed Air-Fried Duck Breast	Teriyaki Glazed Air-Fried Salmon Steaks	Vanilla Cinnamon Air-Fried Pear Slices
Day 7	Low-Carb French Toast Sticks	Cajun Seasoned Air-Fried Shrimp	BBQ Rubbed Air-Fried Pork Ribs	Air-Fried Pineapple Rings with Honey Lime Drizzle
Day 8	Zucchini Fritters	Crispy Coconut-Crusted Air-Fried Cod Fillets	Air-Fried Falafel with Tahini Sauce	Lemon Poppy Seed Air-Fried Muffins
Day 9	Air Fryer Breakfast Sausages	Garlic Parmesan Air-Fried Chicken Wings	Herbed Lemon Air-Fried Swordfish Steaks	Hazelnut Cocoa Air-Fried Granola Clusters
Day 10	Spinach and Feta Egg Muffins	Cajun Spiced Air-Fried Quail	Paprika-Rubbed Air-Fried Beef Sirloin Tips	Pumpkin Spice Air-Fried Sweet Potato Chips
Day 11	Cauliflower Hash Browns	Panko-Crusted Air-Fried Haddock Fillets	Paprika and Rosemary Air-Fried Lamb Chops	Air-Fried Blueberry Almond Crisp
Day 12	Zucchini Fritters	Herbed Pork Tenderloin Medallions	Mediterranean Style Air-Fried Sea Bass	Honey Caramelized Air-Fried Nectarines
Day 13	Almond Flour Pancakes	Buffalo-Style Air-Fried Chicken Tenders	Air-Fried Adzuki Beans with Herbs and Garlic	Chocolate Hazelnut Stuffed Air-Fried Dates
Day 14	Low-Carb Sausage Balls	Teriyaki Glazed Salmon Fillets	Moroccan Spiced Air-Fried Chicken Drumsticks	Air-Fried Raspberry Oatmeal Bars

	Breakfast	**Lunch**	**Dinner**	**Snack/Dessert**
Day 15	Egg and Veggie Breakfast Wraps	Garlic Parmesan Air-Fried Turkey Meatballs	Moroccan Spiced Air-Fried Lamb Kebabs	Maple Cinnamon Air-Fried Plantain Chips
Day 16	Air-Fried Breakfast Quinoa	Air-Fried Italian Sausage with Peppers and Onions	Chili-Lime Air-Fried Shrimp Tacos	Chai Spiced Air-Fried Pears with Greek Yoghurt
Day 17	Turkey and Egg Breakfast Cups	Lemon Pepper Air-Fried Catfish Nuggets	Crispy Air-Fried Coconut Shrimp	Almond Butter Stuffed Air-Fried Apples
Day 18	Low-Carb Cheese and Bacon Biscuits	Jamaican Jerk Air-Fried Pork Tenderloin	Herbed Air-Fried Cornish Hens	Coconut Flour Air-Fried Brownies with Walnuts
Day 19	Crispy Kale Chips	Chili-Lime Air-Fried Chicken Thighs	Blackened Air-Fried Red Snappe	Orange Glazed Air-Fried Peach Slices
Day 20	Breakfast Stuffed Peppers	Coconut Lime Air-Fried Shrimp and Pineapple Skewers	Italian Seasoned Air-Fried Meatballs	Peanut Butter Banana Air-Fried Spring Rolls
Day 21	Coconut Flour Waffles	Chili-Lime Air-Fried Beef Skewers	Maple Mustard Glazed Air-Fried Ham Steaks	Air-Fried Raspberry Oatmeal Bars
Day 22	Aubergine and Tomato Breakfast Stack	BBQ Pulled Chicken Sliders	Honey Mustard Glazed Air-Fried Trout Fillets	Cinnamon Sugar Air-Fried Apple Slices
Day 23	Cottage Cheese Pancakes	Crispy Orange-Glazed Air-Fried Duck Legs	Garlic and Herb Marinated Air-Fried Pork Tenderloin	Chocolate Hazelnut Stuffed Air-Fried Dates
Day 24	Air-Fried Breakfast Potatoes	Cajun Seasoned Air-Fried Crawfish	Mediterranean Style Air-Fried Lentil Patties	Pumpkin Spice Air-Fried Sweet Potato Chips
Day 25	Low-Carb Breakfast Pizza	Spicy Air-Fried Turkey Breast	Parmesan Crusted Air-Fried Oysters	Pumpkin Spice Air-Fried Sweet Potato Chips
Day 26	Cauliflower Hash Browns	Honey Sriracha Air-Fried Chicken Wings	Buffalo-Style Air-Fried Turkey Wings	Air-Fried Banana Chips with Cacao Drizzle
Day 27	Crispy Turkey Bacon	Sriracha-Glazed Air-Fried Mahi-Mahi	Air-Fried Black Bean and Quinoa Burgers	Air-Fried Strawberry Shortcake Skewers
Day 28	Turkey and Egg Breakfast Cups	Lemon Pepper Air-Fried Cod Fillets	Herb-Marinated Air-Fried Scampi	Vanilla Cinnamon Air-Fried Pear Slices
Day 29	Air-Fried Breakfast Quinoa	Air-Fried Spiced Chickpea Stuffed Peppers	Tandoori Chicken Skewers	Chocolate Hazelnut Stuffed Air-Fried Dates
Day 30	Sweet Potato Hash Browns	Crispy Sesame Ginger Air-Fried Tuna Steaks	Mediterranean Style Air-Fried Lamb Burgers	Cinnamon Sugar Air-Fried Apple Slices

INDEX

A

Air-Fried Adzuki Beans with Herbs and Garlic 39
Air-Fried Asparagus Wrapped in Prosciutto 44
Air-Fried Avocado and Egg 10
Air-Fried Banana Chips with Cacao Drizzle 61
Air-Fried Beef and Pepper Skewers 51
Air-Fried Black Bean and Quinoa Burgers 39
Air-Fried Black Bean and Sweet Potato Tacos 42
Air-Fried Blueberry Almond Crisp 63
Air-Fried Breakfast Potatoes 16
Air-Fried Breakfast Quinoa 13
Air-Fried Buffalo Chicken Wings with Greek Yoghurt Ranch Dip 56
Air-Fried Cauliflower Steaks with Herbed Quinoa Pilaf 27
Air-Fried Falafel Patty Burgers 54
Air-Fried Falafel with Tahini Sauce 26, 57
Air-Fried Greek Spanakopita Triangles 60
Air-Fried Honey Mustard Turkey Breast 50
Air-Fried Italian Sausage and Veggie Stir-Fry 52
Air-Fried Italian Sausage with Peppers and Onions 18
Air-Fried Lemon Herb Chicken Breasts 17
Air-Fried Lemon Pepper Chicken Thighs 50
Air-Fried Lentil and Spinach Stuffed Mushrooms 43
Air-Fried Mung Bean Sprouts Salad 40
Air-Fried Pineapple Rings with Honey Lime Drizzle 62
Air-Fried Raspberry Oatmeal Bars 64
Air-Fried Ratatouille Medley 48
Air-Fried Refried Beans with Chipotle 42
Air-Fried Spiced Chickpea Stuffed Peppers 39
Air-Fried Split Pea Falafel with Tahini Sauce 41
Air-Fried Strawberry Shortcake Skewers 61
Air-Fried Stuffed Cherry Tomatoes with Herbed Goat Cheese 59
Air-Fried Stuffed Jalapeño Poppers with Cream Cheese 55
Air-Fried Stuffed Mushrooms with Spinach and Feta 45
Air-Fried Stuffed Peppers with Quinoa and Black Beans 24
Air-Fried Turkey and Spinach Meatballs 53
Air-Fried Veggie Burger Patties with Sweet Potato Fries 27
Air Fryer Breakfast Sausages 11
Air Fryer Veggie Omelette 9
Almond Butter Stuffed Air-Fried Apples 64
Almond Flour Air-Fried Donuts with Sugar-Free Glaze 61
Almond Flour Pancakes 12
Asian-Style Sesame Ginger Air-Fried Beef Stir-Fry 20
Aubergine and Tomato Breakfast Stack 15

B

Balsamic Glazed Air-Fried Aubergine Slices 46
Balsamic Glazed Air-Fried Brussels Sprouts with Cranberries 60
BBQ Pulled Chicken Sliders 21
BBQ Rubbed Air-Fried Pork Loin Slices 50
BBQ Rubbed Air-Fried Pork Ribs 34
Blackened Air-Fried Red Snapper 30
Breakfast Stuffed Peppers 15
Buffalo Cauliflower Bites in the Air Fryer 47
Buffalo Cauliflower Florets in the Air Fryer 51
Buffalo-Style Air-Fried Chicken Tenders 35

Buffalo-Style Air-Fried Turkey Wings   21
Butternut Squash and Chickpea Curry in the Air Fryer   26

C

Cajun Cornbread-Coated Air-Fried Black Eyed Peas   40
Cajun Seasoned Air-Fried Crawfish   31
Cajun Seasoned Air-Fried Shrimp   17
Cajun Spiced Air-Fried Okra Fritters   58
Cajun Spiced Air-Fried Quail   35
Cajun Spiced Air-Fried Shrimp Skewers   28
Caprese-Stuffed Air-Fried Courgette Boats   26
Cauliflower Hash Browns   12
Chai Spiced Air-Fried Pears with Greek Yoghurt   64
Chili-Lime Air-Fried Beef Skewers   36
Chili-Lime Air-Fried Chicken Thighs   19
Chili-Lime Air-Fried Corn on the Cob   45
Chili-Lime Air-Fried Shrimp Tacos   30
Chocolate-Dipped Air-Fried Coconut Macaroons   62
Chocolate Hazelnut Stuffed Air-Fried Dates   63
Cinnamon Apple Chips   10
Cinnamon Sugar Air-Fried Apple Slices   61
Coconut-Crusted Air-Fried Shrimp Cakes   53
Coconut Flour Air-Fried Brownies with Walnuts   65
Coconut Flour Waffles   15
Coconut Lime Air-Fried Shrimp and Pineapple Skewers   32
Cottage Cheese Pancakes   15
Courgette Parmesan in the Air Fryer   25
Crispy Air-Fried Brussels Sprouts with Balsamic Glaze   44
Crispy Air-Fried Butternut Squash Cubes 47
Crispy Air-Fried Coconut Shrimp   23
Crispy Air-Fried Courgette Fries with Yoghurt Dip   55
Crispy Air-Fried Veggie Spring Rolls   50
Crispy Coconut-Crusted Air-Fried Cod Fillets   29
Crispy Coconut Shrimp with Mango Dipping Sauce 56
Crispy Garlic-Parmesan Air-Fried Okra   46
Crispy Garlic Parmesan Air-Fried White Beans   41
Crispy Kale Chips   14
Crispy Onion Rings in the Air Fryer with Spicy Aioli   57
Crispy Orange-Glazed Air-Fried Duck Legs   36
Crispy Parmesan-Rosemary Air-Fried Potatoes   49
Crispy Sesame Ginger Air-Fried Tuna Steaks   32
Crispy Thai-Style Air-Fried Spring Rolls with Dipping Sauce   59
Crispy Tofu and Vegetable Stir-Fry in Air Fryer   25
Crispy Tofu Nuggets in the Air Fryer   52
Crispy Tofu Scramble   12
Crispy Turkey Bacon   9
Crunchy BBQ Seasoned Air-Fried Navy Beans   43

D

Dill and Garlic Air-Fried Squid Rings   33

E

Egg and Veggie Breakfast Wraps   13

G

Garlic and Herb Marinated Air-Fried Pork Tenderloin   22
Garlic Butter Air-Fried Scallops   28
Garlic-Herb Air-Fried Mushrooms Stuffed with Spinach and Cheese   55
Garlic-Herb Air-Fried Parsnip Fries   48
Garlic Parmesan Air-Fried Chicken Wings   18
Garlic Parmesan Air-Fried Crab Cakes   33
Garlic Parmesan Air-Fried Green Beans   44, 59

Garlic Parmesan Air-Fried Turkey Meatballs 35
Garlic-Rosemary Air-Fried Potato Wedges 53

H

Harissa Roasted Air-Fried Lima Beans 41
Hazelnut Cocoa Air-Fried Granola Clusters 63
Herbed Air-Fried Carrot Fries 44
Herbed Air-Fried Chicken Drumettes 51
Herbed Air-Fried Cornish Hens 36
Herbed Air-Fried Potato Skins with Turkey Bacon 58
Herbed Chickpea Fritters in the Air Fryer 41
Herbed Lemon Air-Fried Swordfish Steaks 29
Herbed Pork Tenderloin Medallions 18
Herb-Marinated Air-Fried Cabbage Wedges 49
Herb-Marinated Air-Fried Scampi 32
Herb-Marinated Air-Fried Tomato Slices 46
Honey Caramelized Air-Fried Nectarines 63
Honey Garlic Air-Fried Chicken Thighs 34
Honey Mustard Glazed Air-Fried Pork Chops 20
Honey Mustard Glazed Air-Fried Trout Fillets 31
Honey Sriracha Air-Fried Chicken Wings 37
Honey Sriracha Glazed Air-Fried Carrot Coins 49
Honey Sriracha Glazed Air-Fried Turkey Meatloaf 23

I

Italian Herb Air-Fried Veal Cutlets 37
Italian Seasoned Air-Fried Meatballs 22

J

Jamaican Jerk Air-Fried Chicken Thighs 24
Jamaican Jerk Air-Fried Pork Tenderloin 36

L

Lemon Garlic Air-Fried Cod Fillets 54
Lemon Herb Air-Fried Artichoke Hearts 45
Lemon Herb Air-Fried Avocado Fries 60
Lemon-Herb Air-Fried Mussels 33
Lemon Herb Air-Fried Salmon Steaks 52
Lemon Herb Air-Fried Tilapia Fillets 28
Lemon Herb Air-Fried Turkey Breast 34
Lemon Pepper Air-Fried Artichoke Hearts 56
Lemon Pepper Air-Fried Catfish Nuggets 30
Lemon Pepper Air-Fried Cod Fillets 21
Lemon Pepper Air-Fried Rabbit 38
Lemon-Pepper Air-Fried Sugar Snap Peas 48
Lemon Poppy Seed Air-Fried Muffins 62
Low-Carb Breakfast Burritos 9
Low-Carb Breakfast Pizza 16
Low-Carb Cheese and Bacon Biscuits 14
Low-Carb French Toast Sticks 10
Low-Carb Sausage Balls 13

M

Maple Cinnamon Air-Fried Plantain Chips 64
Maple Mustard Glazed Air-Fried Ham Steaks 36
Mediterranean Style Air-Fried Aubergine Slices 53
Mediterranean Style Air-Fried Falafel with Tahini Sauce 57
Mediterranean Style Air-Fried Green Bean Salad 49
Mediterranean Style Air-Fried Lamb Burgers 37
Mediterranean Style Air-Fried Lamb Kebabs 20
Mediterranean Style Air-Fried Lentil Patties 39
Mediterranean Style Air-Fried Sea Bass 29
Mexican-Style Air-Fried Stuffed Poblano Peppers 27
Moroccan Spiced Air-Fried Chicken Drumsticks 23
Moroccan Spiced Air-Fried Lamb Kebabs 35

O

Orange Glazed Air-Fried Peach Slices   65

P

Panko-Crusted Air-Fried Courgette Chips 45
Panko-Crusted Air-Fried Haddock Fillets 29
Paprika and Cumin Spiced Air-Fried Lamb Chops 19
Paprika and Rosemary Air-Fried Lamb Chops 35
Paprika Roasted Air-Fried Broccoli Florets 45
Paprika-Rubbed Air-Fried Beef Sirloin Tips 24
Parmesan Crusted Air-Fried Acorn Squash Rings 46
Parmesan-Crusted Air-Fried Cauliflower Bites 55
Parmesan Crusted Air-Fried Oysters   31
Parmesan-Herb Air-Fried Tilapia Fillets   51
Peanut Butter Banana Air-Fried Spring Rolls 65
Pesto Marinated Air-Fried Cannellini Beans 42
Pesto Marinated Air-Fried Chicken Drumsticks   38
Pesto Marinated Air-Fried Shrimp Scampi 52
Pesto Mozzarella-Stuffed Air-Fried Portobello Mushrooms   59
Pumpkin Spice Air-Fried Sweet Potato Chips 63

R

Rosemary and Garlic Air-Fried Steak   19
Rosemary and Lemon Air-Fried Chickpea Salad 43
Rosemary Balsamic Air-Fried Beef Roast 37
Rosemary Roasted Air-Fried Pepper Strips 47

S

Sesame Ginger Air-Fried Bok Choy   48
Sesame Ginger Air-Fried Turkey Burgers 38
Sesame Soy Air-Fried Soybean Sprouts   42
Smoky Paprika Air-Fried Kidney Beans   40
Soy-Garlic Marinated Air-Fried Pork Belly Slices 38
Spicy Air-Fried Turkey Breast   21
Spicy Chipotle Air-Fried Lobster Tails   33
Spicy Curry Air-Fried Adzuki Bean Snack 43
Spicy Soy-Glazed Air-Fried Tofu Cubes 54
Spicy Sriracha Air-Fried Tofu Bites   57
Spinach and Feta Egg Muffins   11
Spinach and Mushroom Stuffed Portobello Mushrooms   25
Sriracha-Glazed Air-Fried Mahi-Mahi   31
Sweet Potato Hash Browns 10

T

Tandoori Chicken Skewers 22
Teriyaki Glazed Air-Fried Duck Breast   34
Teriyaki Glazed Air-Fried Meatballs   58
Teriyaki Glazed Air-Fried Salmon Steaks 28
Teriyaki Glazed Air-Fried Tofu Steaks   50
Teriyaki Glazed Salmon Fillets   18
Turkey and Egg Breakfast Cups   14
Turkey Meatballs with Marinara Sauce   17
Turmeric and Cumin Roasted Air-Fried Radishes   47
Turmeric and Cumin Spiced Air-Fried Falafel 40
Turmeric Spiced Air-Fried Cauliflower Steaks 44

V

Vanilla Cinnamon Air-Fried Pear Slices 62

Z

Zucchini Fritters   11

Printed in Great Britain
by Amazon